THE TAO OF DATING

The Smart Woman's Guide to
Embracing Your Inner Goddess and
Finding the Fulfillment You Deserve

Alex Benzer, M.D., M.Phil.
www.taoofdating.com

To Mom and Dad, to whom I owe everything
To all my teachers, to whom I owe everything else

Before you proceed any further – make sure you claim your bonus download material!

Those who purchase this book or ebook online get a number of digital download bonuses, including:

• An audio download of the popular Galactic Consciousness Meditation and several other exercises from the book
• An audio download and 26-page transcript of the *How to Be A Modern Goddess* teleseminar of January 2009, which is new material not covered in the book
• A free electronic subscription to the *Tao of Dating* articles, where I address the questions that are just too hot for the blog
• A little surprise bonus that I can't tell about, because then it wouldn't be a surprise anymore

These bonuses are designed to enhance and complement the material in the book. The guided meditation audios are particularly powerful, since they allow you to experience the meditations with your eyes closed.

I want to make sure you have a chance to get the same bonuses as the online purchasers. So go ahead and visit this page now to claim your digital downloads:

www.taoofdating.com/goddess

Acknowledgments

Writing a book for women when you're a guy is tougher than I thought. Which is why I'm deeply indebted to my illustrious panel of readers who provided invaluable feedback. Alexis, Aiko, Cristina, Naada, and Sharon – you are all stars. Alison and Megan – thank you for your particularly thorough look at the manuscript and your dozens of great suggestions. Special thanks to Christine Mason McCaull for suggesting the addition of several sections which made the book stronger and for allowing me to use her 'Love your body now' piece.

I also want to thank my loyal readers who encouraged me through their emails to keep on writing. This project could not have been completed without you.

Profuse thanks to my talented and highly responsive graphic designer Thomas Breher for his work on the cover. You can find him at eCoverDesign.com. Tell him I sent you.

There are always shadow mentors in the background of every project, and the Rev. Dr. Michael Bernard Beckwith of the Agape Transdenominational Spiritual Center has been one of them. For many years, his uplifting words have provided much-needed fuel in times of uncertainty. His teachings are an integral part of this book.

And finally, I'd like to thank Mom & Dad for their unfailing support. This book is for you.

About the author

Dr Alex holds an A.B. from Harvard College, an M.D. from the University of California San Diego School of Medicine, and an M.Phil. from Cambridge University. He is a Certified Clinical Hypnotherapist and NLP Master Practitioner. He has consulted for Fortune 100 companies and maintains a hypnotherapy practice in Los Angeles, California. He is committed to helping you become the best possible version of you.

TABLE OF CONTENTS

The Introduction You Can't Skip

PART I: THE WAY: FOUNDATIONS OF THE TAO

Chapter 1: Dating for Fulfillment

Chapter 2: Who You Really Are

Chapter 3: Yin and Yang

Chapter 4: What You Really Want

Chapter 5: Understanding Men, Understanding Yourself

PART II: BE

Chapter 6: Beliefs

Chapter 7: Attitudes

PART III: DO

Chapter 8: Find

Chapter 9: Meet

Chapter 10: Attract

Chapter 11: Romance, or what to do on a date

PART IV: HAVE

Chapter 12: Have: Making Relationships Last

Chapter 13: A New Beginning

There was something formless and perfect
before the universe was born.
It is serene. Empty.
Solitary. Unchanging.
Infinite. Eternally present.
It is the mother of the universe.
For lack of a better name,
I call it the Tao.

It flows through all things,
Inside and outside, and returns
To the origin of all things.

The Tao is great.
The universe is great.
Earth is great.
Man is great.
These are the four great powers.

Man follows the earth.
Earth follows the universe.
The universe follows the Tao.
The Tao follows only itself.

– Lao Tzu, Tao Te Ching, *Ch. 25, transl. Stephen Mitchell*

.

The Introduction You Can't Skip

Monica's story, or how this book got started

It was one of those early fall Boston days a few years ago when you thought anything was possible. The sky was unusually clear, the air was crisp, and Newbury Street was humming with life and brimming with attractive people. I was excited about meeting up with my college classmate Monica, whom I had not seen since we had both graduated from Harvard.

You probably know Monica, or someone like her. She is smart, good-looking, funny, in great shape, well-read, stylish, successful – the total package. She had her act together – so much so that guys in college had been almost too intimidated to ask her out.

We met at the sidewalk café Sonsie to catch up. And as we discussed work, family, friends, and love life, the question came up: "So – you seeing anyone?"

There was a shifting in the chair, a looking away, and Monica mumbled, "Well, no, not really." Now, normally that's not a remarkable fact. But Monica is kind of a remarkable woman. Some might even say a serious babe. If *she* was perpetually single, something must have been seriously wrong with the world.

Then I started having conversations like that one with other female friends, and a pattern started to emerge. Talented, educated, attractive women were having unfulfilling dating lives on an epidemic scale. They either couldn't find the right guy, were with the wrong guy, had relationships that didn't last, or had given up entirely on the whole dating business.

This came to me as a surprise. I mean, these were all exceptional women. There should have been a line of fantastic guys around the block for any one of them. And yet, they were alone. And lonely. Surely something was terribly wrong with the world.

So I had to ask – what's going on here? That's when I thought there may be a need for a dating guide specifically geared for smart professional women.

A guy, writing a dating book for women?

As it turns out, my guy classmates were having similar issues, so I started out by writing the book for men, which I finished in three intense months of writing and research in 2005. The book was well-received, and in late 2006, I set out to write the *Tao of Dating* for women, thinking that it would take about the same amount of time. Piece of cake, right? *Wrong*. Turns out it's not as easy as I thought to write a dating book for women when you're not a woman.

I was seriously stuck for a long time. More than once I considered abandoning the project. I mean, what does a guy know about the inner lives of women anyway? Surely there were 3 billion people out there better-qualified to write this book[1].

In the meantime, because of the success of the men's book, I was getting daily letters from men about *their* dating woes. And they were having said woes with women, shockingly enough. Little by little, from these thousands of men, a database started to emerge: what they really liked, what they didn't like so much, and what absolutely sent them

---

[1] That would be the female half of the world's population.

running for the hills. As their confidante, I also became privy to their innermost thoughts desires, and schemes. Could *this* be of interest to my female readers? Perhaps.

Holly's story, or how this book got finished

Then, something else happened. Fast-forward to 2008. The book is still slogging along, and I was visiting Boston, having relocated to Los Angeles in the interim. I was having dinner with two of my college classmates, Ariela and Holly. Both are professional women in their thirties, both charming, sweet, fabulous-looking and divorced. Ariela is single without kids; Holly has a daughter and is seeing someone. Let's call him Tim. Ariela clearly does not approve of Tim, so I decide to get the full story.

"Tell me about this guy," I ask Holly.

She responds, "Well, he's really tall and handsome; the sex is great; he's really sweet most of the time; he's a bit of the starving-artist type, and he's not as successful as I am, so I've been supporting him for the past couple of years."

So far, so bad. I sensed she was holding back, and called her on it. And – really sweet *most* of the time? What's up with *that*?

"Well, when we first met he was just such a sweetheart. But lately he's been sniping at me, putting me down for no reason. And when I spend time with my friends he gets really jealous and makes me feel guilty."

"Tell him what happened when your daughter fell down the stairs," said Ariela with a fire of barely concealed rage in her eyes.

Holly hesitated. "Well, last month my daughter fell down the stairs at home and cut her head open. There was blood everywhere, and we rushed her to the hospital. I was so shaken, and I just needed Tim to be by my side, so I called him up. He didn't come."

Didn't come? Just like that? And you're still dating this dude?

"He said he was afraid of blood, and he just couldn't deal with the situation."

My heart sank. How was this possible? Why was this amazing woman wasting another minute of her life on this unworthy man? What else is happening that she's not sharing with us? How many other women like her were stuck in the same place?

At this point, Ariela and I made a very clear case for why Holly needed to break it off with this guy immediately. Then Ariela looked me in the eye and held my right forearm for emphasis: "Alex, you have a duty to finish this book as quickly as possible."

I realized that if my book could help even one woman like Holly (and Monica) reclaim their power, then I had to complete it and bring it to light. Two months after that talk, I finished *The Tao of Dating*. And Holly asked Tim (who turns out was also physically abusing her) to move out and never contact her again, not a minute too soon.

A dating guide for the modern smart, professional, educated woman

Although Monica and Holly were just two of the women amongst the dozens I spoke to, their cases were not unique. Their stories all shared common themes.

For most of the women there were external circumstances such as focus on their careers that accounted for part of what was happening. But I was also hearing excuses from them that didn't make a lot of sense: "There aren't any good men." "I don't have time to meet people." "I'm an old-fashioned girl – dating's just not my thing." Or the worst, from those who were dating the wrong guy: "But he's nice *sometimes*."

Some of them genuinely didn't know how to date effectively. And they weren't entirely at fault: the rules of dating are unwritten, and no one had bothered to teach any of us what they might be. But even more important, I witnessed that they had abdicated their own power as women and people. While I saw them as tremendously attractive, magnetic individuals that any man would be lucky to associate with, they did not. As a result, they ended up alone or with the wrong guy.

So this book has two objectives: to help educated, intelligent, discriminating women get back their personal power in the dating arena and beyond; and to give them some solid strategies for realizing a fulfilling dating life. As a man, I wish to provide a fresh perspective on women's strength and beauty that they may have forgotten themselves and also provide the man's perspective on which dating strategies work best.

Since writing *The Tao of Dating For Men* three years ago, I have been privy to hundreds of stories of men's challenges relating to women. I combined that with my own experiences to give you a sense of what works best with educated, intelligent, successful men of integrity when it comes to dating. As a hypnotherapist, seminar leader and personal success consultant, I want to give you tools to re-claim your personal power in all areas of your life. If you're reading this book, chances are you are a remarkable woman, and I want to make sure you remember that. Think of this book as what a big brother with your best interest at heart would tell you if he had a thorough knowledge of the male psyche and had experienced several dates himself. Seeing you happy makes me happy.

Some time ago, I was introduced to Taoist philosophy and found much wisdom in its lighthearted yet practical way of viewing the world. As its title suggests, this book draws on

Taoist philosophy, which arises from observation of the way the world works. As such, it is more about the way things are, rather than the way things should be – more descriptive than prescriptive, more empirical than theoretical. Like Taoism, there is no doctrine, no dogma, and few rules. In fact, at every point, I encourage you to test the ideas and find out how well they work for you instead of blindly accepting them at face value. If it works for you, keep it. If it doesn't, toss it and try something else.

Like the teachings of the Eastern masters and the *Tao Te Ching*, the concepts may seem paradoxical at first. I urge you to find the hidden truth behind the paradox. You may also find that some of these ideas go directly against your expectations or beliefs. In those cases, I encourage you to just test them out, without any prejudice as to whether they are right or wrong: just see what happens. As Albert Einstein said, "If at first the idea is not absurd, then there is no hope for it." Ordinary ideas and measures will give you ordinary results at best. Extraordinary results, on the other hand, require extraordinary measures. As such, the more an idea challenges your current belief set, the more likely it is to effect breakthrough in your life.

You should think of the ideas in this book as tools for achieving whatever your dating goals may be, from a fling to marriage. I've based these concepts in ancient wisdom along with proven science to ensure that they are as timeless and universal as possible – as likely to be true a hundred years from now as they are today. As such, although the book is based on a North American model of dating, most of the principles are applicable regardless of who or where you are. At the same time, I make some assumptions about you, the reader:

1) You are interested in long-term fulfillment as opposed to short-term gain. There are two operating

words here: *long-term* and *fulfillment*. As with investment and career choices, the tactics for short-term gain in dating tend to be different from the ones for long-term benefit. Also, it's important to remember that fulfillment is not a person – it is a feeling. And sometimes the way to have that fulfillment will seem paradoxical (e.g. spending some quality time alone).

2) For the purposes of long-term relationships, you are interested first and foremost in a Good Guy. A Good Guy is a man (as opposed to a boy) who knows what he wants and knows where he's going. He has a strong internal compass guiding him along his life's purpose, he's completely comfortable in his own skin, and he's a leader. At the same time that he's a perfect gentleman, always having your well-being in mind, he's perfectly willing to give you some gentle ribbing every once in a while. He exists in contradistinction to such male archetypes as the Bad Boy, Man-Child and Nice (But Kind of Wimpy) Guy.

3) You are open both to scientific concepts and spiritual principles and are willing to try on novel ideas that are likely to bring more fun and fulfillment into your life. If you're more scientifically-oriented, consider this an introduction to spiritual concepts. If you're more spiritually-oriented, consider this a chance to delve into your scientific side.

In the end, this book is more about helping you find your own way than about telling you what to do. Sometimes we can get stuck in a rut, and all it takes is a tiny jolt, a little piece of information, to get us up and running again. Many people are finding that jolt amongst the precepts of Eastern wisdom, and if you're reading this, it's likely that you are one of them.

Some of you will find *The Tao of Dating* highly applicable to where you are and where you want to be, and some perhaps less so. As for me – I have been through 21 years of formal education, attended countless lectures and gone through thousands of books in my lifetime. It's safe to say that I have not used 100% of everything that I have learned. But I still seek out new sources of information, sit through weekend-long seminars and sift through new books. Even if I get *one* new idea, *one* mental shift to see something in a new way, *one* re-iteration of a key concept that I had forgotten, or *one* new application of a concept, then that exercise has been worthwhile. I urge you to look at any new learning experience in that way, including this book. New concepts sometimes take time to digest and results may be subtle at first, so go easy on yourself.

One spark is sometimes all it takes to start a raging fire, and I sincerely hope that you will find many sparks in the time you spend with this book. I congratulate you on making the decision to bring the Tao into your life today. Once you allow it, you will find that it will empower you and change your life in ways you had not imagined before.

The five themes of *The Tao of Dating*

This book is organized around five overarching themes. We will go over each one in detail in the book, but I want to prime your mind so you pay closer attention each time they appear:

• The first is *wealth-consciousness*, or the mindset of abundance. There is enough of everything to go around for everyone.

• The second is the *Be-Do-Have mentality*, which relates to Napoleon Hill's famous saying from *Think and Grow Rich*: "Whatever the mind of man can conceive and believe, it can achieve."

• The third is *enlightened self-interest*, which is about acting with your long-term well-being in mind.

• The fourth is *feminine-masculine (yin-yang) polarity*.

• The fifth is *getting out of your own way*.

How to use this book

The purpose of *The Tao of Dating* is not just to give you some tricks and hints for you to scrape by on, but rather to turn you into the most empowered, fulfilled version of you possible. As such, this book is equally about *transformation* and information. In order to effect that transformation, you have to apply the principles in the book to your life.

So I want you to approach this book less as a novel that you read once and shelve and more like a handbook, travel guide or cookbook. Mark up the chapters and exercises that you like and come back to them. I've read the *Tao Te Ching* at least 300 times, and I keep on coming back to it, just because something in there always provides me with a new perspective on what's happening. Think of this book in that vein – a reference you will keep on coming back to.

Now if you're like most people, you are probably going to start reading the book, get to an exercise, skip it, and go straight to the juicy parts about tips and tricks. So go ahead and do that – I won't tell anyone. Skim the book once from beginning to end. Then go back and *do the exercises*.

That is where the transformation occurs (and where some of the tips and tricks are hidden).

The Tao of Dating contains a lot of information. If you attempt to remember and try out every idea at once, it may be overwhelming. That is why the book is organized in a linear fashion. Start from the beginning, from the work on values, beliefs, attitudes and what you want. Then move on to the section on how to find quality men. Progress stepwise to meeting men, attracting them, and perpetuating your relationships with them.

Think of it as baking bread. If you've never done it before, you start by thinking about a recipe. You then go through each step of making the bread in order: go to store, buy ingredients, mix them, make dough, bake, eat. If you try to do everything at once, you're more likely to end up with a mess in the kitchen than an edible loaf. But if you proceed sequentially, at every step of the way you just have to remember what the next step is. As Lao Tzu says, "The journey of a thousand miles begins with a single step." Go easy, and good fortune.

I'm very interested in your thoughts about this book, so do me a favor and drop a line sometime. Just put 'Question', or 'Comment' or 'That was awesome can I buy you a drink' in the subject line of your email so I know to pay special attention to it. You can write to me personally at:

dralex(at)taoofdating.com

Part I
The Way:
Foundations of
the Tao

道

Chapter 1. Dating for Fulfillment

Which would you prefer: the menu or the food?

Imagine that you're hungry right now at a diner. And they offer you just the menu but no food. Would you settle for that? Or would you demand actual food?

That may seem like a silly question. But in real life, people sometimes operate as if they aren't sure about the answer. They chase down the symbol representing what we want – money, titles – instead of the actual thing that we want. But the money and the titles are only as good as the feelings and experiences they can get for us.

So while reading this book, I'd like you to keep in mind what constitutes real fulfillment for you in the dating realm – the actual food, not the menu. Because fulfillment is not a person – it's a feeling. The right person is the one who catalyzes an abundance of fulfilling feelings in your life, like love, peace and contentment. If you're not getting those feelings, it may be a sign that you're either with the wrong person or that you could approach matters with an even better perspective.

Square one: accept and love yourself now

Some argue that the ultimate aim of everything we do in life is to get more love. You could be reading this book because you want more love from men, more love from your friends, or more love from yourself. Of those three, only one is directly under your control – the love you have for yourself. Generally speaking, being better with men won't make your friends like you any better (and sometimes may have the opposite effect). And chances are that if you are not happy with yourself right now, no amount of success with men will ever make up for that. And no man will be able to trigger feelings of fulfillment in you.

In fact, it only gets harder when you *have* what you *thought* would make you happy and still find happiness elusive. So go ahead and decide *now* to be comfortable in your own skin and to accept yourself exactly as you are. Why? Besides being a good starting point, there is no time when it's not right now. Now is the only time. And true fulfillment can only come from sharing your joy, contentment and self-sufficiency with the rest of the world in the present moment. Decide it, claim it, be it.

> *...If you look to others for fulfillment,*
> *you will never truly be fulfilled.*
> *If your happiness depends on money,*
> *you will never be happy with yourself.*

Chapter 1. Dating for Fulfillment

Be content with what you have;
rejoice in the way things are.
When you realize there is nothing lacking,
the whole world belongs to you.

  — Lao Tzu, Tao Te Ching, Ch. 44

So if you're perfectly okay right where you are, why would you need this book? Great question. It reminds me of an old Buddhist saying: "We are perfect as we are, and we could all use a little work."

Here's one way to think about it. Seeking out resources for self-improvement simply means that you are on a journey of growth. And in order to reach your goals in dating – or anything else in life – it's important to believe that at every point along this journey of growth, you are complete. A sequoia seedling is always a sequoia at every point along its path to becoming a towering tree. And so are you always an empowered, fulfilled woman on your way to even greater empowerment and fulfillment. You are always turning into the best possible version of you.

This is important because the world tends to be a reflection of your dominant thoughts. When you signal to the world "I am okay," the world will agree with you. When you signal "Well, I'll be okay if I just get this little part fixed, but I'm not quite okay right now," then the world will agree with you also.

Recognize that whatever mindset you have right now is the one you're likely to carry with you for the rest of your life. If you don't think you're okay right now, chances are that no events or circumstances will change that. Thus I encourage you to choose right now to adopt the mindset that, wherever you are, regardless of your real or imagined inadequacies, you accept yourself just as you are. Stop the

29

struggle and just be. Chapter 29 of the *Tao Te Ching* puts it thus:

> *Do you want to improve the world?*
> *I don't think it can be done.*
>
> *The world is sacred.*
> *It can't be improved.*
> *If you tamper with it, you'll ruin it.*
> *If you treat it like an object, you'll lose it.*
>
> *There is a time for being ahead,*
> *A time for being behind;*
> *A time for being in motion,*
> *A time for being at rest;*
> *A time for being vigorous,*
> *A time for being exhausted;*
> *A time for being safe,*
> *A time for being in danger.*
>
> *The Master sees things as they are,*
> *without trying to control them.*
> *She lets them go their own way,*
> *and resides at the center of the circle.*

Fulfillment is a feeling, not a person

The most common question I get from my readers is *"How do I get this guy?"* The answer is simple: you're asking the wrong question.

Deep down, women seek relationships not because they want a particular guy, but rather because they want the feelings that a good relationship brings them. This class of feelings I call *fulfillment*. Fulfillment is having someone to see that movie with, someone to cook dinner for (or to cook for you), someone to take with you to your best friend's wedding, someone to cuddle up with on a Friday night.

A big mistake in relationships is focusing on the person instead of the fulfillment. The object of your desire could be the most exceptional man on earth, but if he lives 5 hours away or is a workaholic and is never around when you want his company, chances are you are not going to be fulfilled in the long run.

When you are dating someone, ask yourself often, "Do I feel fulfilled in this relationship?" and answer that question with utter honesty. If the answer is 'no' at any point, you may wish to reconsider your situation. The flip side of that is when you *do* feel fulfilled for the most part, but there are some points of conflict looming in your mind. In that case, you may wish to weigh the relative importance of those peccadilloes compared to the fulfillment you're already experiencing.

Another issue with seeking out a particular man as the key to your fulfillment is that by doing so, you are denying the abundance of the world. When you chase anything in life, you are affirming its lack in your life. Spiritual law holds that the world tends to mirror your dominant thoughts. So if you affirm the lack of something in your life, be it wealth, companionship or health, the world will agree with you, and that thing will be driven farther away from your reach. We'll discuss this topic further in Chapter 5 on Beliefs.

Now one sure way to chase away your own fulfillment is to compare yourself to others: Jane has a better-looking, better-educated boyfriend who cooks for her; Barbara's boyfriend is marriage-minded, etc. Comparison gets you in trouble because comparing yourself with those whom you perceive as better off can make you bitter. Comparison with those whom you perceive as worse off can make you vain (and frankly, bitter and vain people are a bit of a drag to be around). If you're ever going to compare, compare yourself to your former self, and notice how far you have come along. And stay centered on your fulfillment, which will be different from that of anyone else.

The power of gratitude

So what constitutes a more effective approach than wishing, wanting, needing, and yearning your way into a fulfilling relationship? The secret weapon here is called gratitude. The idea is simple: right now, if you are sitting somewhere and reading this book, chances are you have a roof over your head and are clothed and fed. You probably have a job and friends and family who care for you. Trillions of cellular operations are all working in harmony this very second to keep you alive and functioning. There is *no end* to the things you could be grateful for.

Of course, you have a choice. You could focus on what's missing from your life – a 70-ft yacht on the French Riviera, a villa in Tuscany or a doting, movie-star boyfriend or husband. Or you can focus on the infinitude of things that are *right* with your life (and there are billions of them, I assure you). Focusing on the billions of things that are right with your life is more likely to make you feel good than focusing on the few things that you perceive as missing. Try this fun little exercise to get a better sense of what I mean.

Exercise 1. The Power of Focus
Take about 30 seconds right now to look around the room. Take notice and mentally catalog everything in the room that is *brown*, and do your best to remember as many of them as possible. Look around and do that now; when you are done, continue reading.

> Now, while keeping your eye on the page, recall all the items in the room that are *green*. Green? Yes, green. You probably didn't come up with many, since you were so focused on the brown stuff. You tend to get more of what you focus on. So choose to focus on the good stuff, and you'll have no choice but to get more of it.

Gratitude feels good. Gratitude may be the most empowering feeling you can have. And it's always there, even when you think it isn't. All you have to do is to choose to focus on what's good in your life. In his moving book *Man's Search for Meaning*, Viktor Frankl recounts how even in the midst of the unimaginable brutality of a Nazi concentration camp, he was able to find things to be grateful for: the companionship of his friends in camp; a moment of solitude; the savoring of a dry morsel of bread. So when you're feeling down, it can be helpful to remind yourself of how good you really do have it compared to what could be.

You can even feel gratitude for the relationship that you would like to have. The fact is that the person with whom you'll be sharing this relationship is already out there somewhere, and it's only a matter of time before you meet or recognize him. Think of it as a paycheck that you've already worked for and is coming to you sooner or later; you're sure it's coming, just not exactly *when* it's coming. And you're okay with that.

When you feel gratitude, you feel good, and when you feel good, you glow. Other people will gravitate towards you. There is no more attractive force than being an epicenter of positive feeling. So gratitude becomes the magnet that will draw the right person into your life. As Tenzin Gyatso, the 13th Dalai Lama famously noted, "There is no way to happiness; happiness is the way."

Another neat feature of gratitude is that it tends to be its own reward. Feelings don't come with little color-coded flags saying *this is the name of what you are feeling.* For example, what you may think of as fear you could just as easily re-interpret as excitement or anticipation. Similarly, gratitude feels a lot like fulfillment; in fact, it may be the essence of what fulfillment is. So when you consciously choose to feel gratitude, you're bringing fulfillment into your life on demand. And when you have that feeling of fulfillment and the empowerment that comes with it, you may no longer feel that you really *need* a man, since you already have the feelings that he would bring. However, you may still *want* a man, which is a much more empowered position to operate from than needing one. More on that later.

The Be-Do-Have Paradigm

Most people are seeking some kind of result in life, and believe that success means *having* that result, be it wealth, status, relationships. As such, they're often looking for the shortcut, the quick and dirty solution, the overnight scheme. Sure, there are overnight schemes; the problem is that they also tend to last only overnight. Easy come, easy go.

True success, on the other hand, is not an accident; it is a *habit.* Most lottery winners go back to their original or lower level of wealth just two years after winning all that money; many go bankrupt. True success only comes from embarking on a path of mastery, which takes time and effort. By purchasing this book and reading this far, you have taken the first and second steps on that path. For that I congratulate you. Seventy percent of people don't even make it this far[*]. Keep up the good work.

---

[*] And 82% of all statistics are made up right on the spot. Ha.

34

Most people think of success in terms of possession: in order to *be* someone, you must *have* something. If you have money and spend lots of it, you are rich. If you have an attractive mate, you are successful in dating.

The truth is that the *reverse* of this mindset is the true key to success. All great works of spirituality from the *Tao Te Ching* to the Bible emphasize that the first step of success is to embody the vision of the success you want to have: "As you believe, so it is done unto you." A simple and powerful articulation of this is the Be-Do-Have paradigm, in which success comes from possessing the mindset, "I am a successful person." This in turn leads to actions. The actions then manifest the signs that people commonly refer to as success.

There is a long-standing tradition in Eastern wisdom of being detached from results. As Krishna said to Arjuna in the *Bhagavad Gita*, you are entitled to your actions, not the results of your actions. Here's the insight: if you are following the path of fulfillment, then the *action is the result*. The work is the wealth. As Mahatma Gandhi put it, "Full effort is full victory."

Let's use the example of money. In order to be wealthy, first you must *be* a wealthy person, with the attendant mindsets and beliefs. You wake up in the morning thinking, "How would Warren Buffett spend his day?" Once you have convinced your brain that you are a wealthy person, then you will naturally *do* what a wealthy person does – do your homework, make good decisions, have shrewd associates, be thrifty in your ways, have overall welfare in mind. And, as a result, not only will you effortlessly *have* what a wealthy person possesses, but you will also have the true wealth of following a path of fulfillment. This is true of any sphere of endeavor.

You rise to a higher level of consciousness by taking your attention away from your present limitations and placing it upon that which you desire to be. Do not attempt this in day-dreaming or wishful thinking but in a positive manner. Claim yourself to be the thing desired. I AM that; no sacrifice, no diet, no human tricks. All that is asked of you is to accept your desire. If you dare claim it, you will express it.
— *Neville*, Your Faith Is Your Fortune

For example, Marie Curie was always the brilliant Nobel-winning scientist, even when she was a young, penniless nanny. When she inhabited that 18-year old mind and body without access to knowledge of her future, she may have never imagined turning into one of the greatest scientists in history and the winner of two Nobel prizes. Yet to us, it seems strange to think of her any other way than *the* Marie Curie, regardless of her age. You can apply that example to the young versions of any great person in history. The young Eleanor Roosevelt, Jane Austen, and Indira Gandhi all harbored self-doubt in their development towards greatness. Yet, in retrospect, they were great to us even as young women on the journey. Recognize that you are on that same journey of greatness, and that it takes a little bit of time for the greatness to fully manifest.

So now I invite you to envision the most brilliant vision of your future. Where do you see yourself in 10 years? In twenty? What will you accomplish? How do you want to be remembered? What kind of relationships will you have? With what kind of people? Make that vision as grand as possible, and then start to embody it immediately. Re-read the quote from Neville above. Is there a guarantee that all the details of your vision will come true? Perhaps not 100%.

But *without* the vision, there is hardly a chance of achieving the goal.

So dare to think and imagine. No one has access to your thoughts, so make them as big and brilliant and inspiring as possible. Great thoughts cost as much as mediocre ones, so might as well go big. Now is a good time to do the following exercise.

Exercise 2. Your highest vision of yourself

Take a deep breath and close your eyes. Imagine yourself as a child, maybe 7 years old. Remember then how badly you wanted to grow up, be tall, go places like the grownups, reach high shelves, drive a car. Remember that feeling of inadequacy that you had then and how you just couldn't wait for all this to happen.

Now bring a picture of your current adult self into the scene, and give your child self a big hug saying, "Hey, told you it was all going to be all right." Feel that deep compassion and acceptance.

Now imagine a third version of yourself – a version from the future that embodies all the accomplishments and goals you are seeking right now. What does that person look like? Really take the time to notice her voice, her gait, her demeanor. How does she look and sound? How does it feel to be her? Now have that future you come in and give the present you a big hug, saying "It's all going to be all right," just the way you hugged the 7-year old you.

Now let the three pictures of you from the past, present and the future merge into one another, leaving an image of that highest vision of yourself, and realize that it is you, right now. When you feel the empowering feelings that brings, squeeze your left fist twice. From now on, all you have to do to bring that empowering feeling back is to repeat that double squeeze.

In this chapter, we will break down the Be-Do-Have paradigm into four practical components: right beliefs, leading to right attitudes, leading to right behaviors, which naturally flow into right results. The steps go from the more hidden to the more manifest. Beliefs and attitudes are the *be* phase; attitudes and behaviors are the *do* phase; results are the *have* phase.

Beliefs are completely hidden, not even manifest to the trained eye. Since your beliefs are yours to know alone, it makes sense to have the most effective beliefs possible, as grandiose or foolhardy as they may sound. Strong, empowering beliefs cost as much as mediocre, ineffective ones: they're all free![2] So use the beliefs that serve you best.

An *attitude* is the first-level manifestation of a belief, hardly detectable even to a trained observer. Sometimes it is expressed verbally or in body language; other times it manifests itself as the subtext of behavior. People tend to respond not to your hidden thoughts or to your manifest behavior, but rather to your overall attitude. Your attitude is the meta-message and meaning of your behavior.

Behavior is what you do, which is easy to observe. The range of possible behaviors is infinite, yet most of us operate within a narrow envelope of behavior which those who know us call our personality. When we do something that seems to breach that narrow envelope, they say that we are behaving 'out of character.' Behavioral range is determined by attitudes and beliefs. It is possible to change attitudes and beliefs by

---

[2] Didn't I just say that? Yes I did. And I'll say it again, because it's so important: as long as all thoughts are free, choose to think the positive, empowering ones. Feeling good, like feeling crappy, is mostly a choice.

regularly engaging in new behaviors consistent with those new beliefs.

Results are the most manifest component of the process. Results broadcast themselves just fine yet reveal little useful information regarding how to achieve them. Knowing how much wealth someone has does not help you get rich like them; nor does seeing that someone has a wonderful companion tell you how that came about. This may seem obvious, but most people find themselves motivated by observing the results and not the process by which they came into being. So henceforth, in all spheres of life, wherever you observe success, look at the *process*. That is where the true wealth resides.

> *The soft overcomes the hard.*
> *The slow overcomes the fast.*
> *Let your workings remain a mystery.*
> *Just show people the results.*
> — *Lao Tzu*, Tao Te Ching, *Ch. 36*

Affective forecasting, or what *really* happens when you get what you want

We humans are hypersocial beings, and companionship is an essential part of our experience. But, come to think of it, you don't really *need* a man in your life. Not the same way you need food, water, shelter, clothing, oxygen and Vitamin D; they are essential to your survival and health. Now you may *want* a man, and that's okay (and in any case, men are much more flattered when they are wanted rather than needed).

However, a man is not a panacea. If you're in a bad job situation, don't get along with your family, have financial troubles, or fundamentally aren't happy with yourself, a man in your life is not likely to solve those issues, no matter how fantastic he is. A man can at best be a conduit and catalyst for feelings of fulfillment. Keep in mind especially that all feelings that you have, *you* generate inside your head. There is no wire from the outside world that plugs into the back of your head and makes you have feelings. If there is one person in the world chiefly responsible for your feelings, it's you.

Daniel Gilbert of Harvard studies *affective forecasting*, our ability to predict how we will feel in the future in response to events. What he has found is that, a few months down the road from the event, we don't feel nearly as good as we thought we would about pleasant things, nor feel nearly as bad about negative ones. In other words, we overestimate both our happiness and distress in response to future events. A year after an event, we tend to return to the same baseline level of happiness we had before.

Finding a suitable male companion may be likened to winning the lottery. Most women desirous of a relationship think they would be *really* happy if they started dating a wonderful man, in the same way that most people think they'd be really happy if they won a lottery. The fact is, soon after winning a lottery, the winners tend to return to the baseline level of happiness they had before winning. It's reasonable to conclude that the level of contentment and happiness you feel, after the initial whirlwind of excitement in a relationship has settled, is the same as the one you are experiencing right now in your seat while reading this passage.

There is a spiritual principle in operation here, reiterated in many guises in numerous traditions, but its essence is this: *You have everything that you need.* Right here, right now. Now this may be challenging to grasp, as you wonder about unpaid bills, an empty fridge and all that extra room in your bed at night. But at a deep and fundamental level, it is always true. At every point in your life leading to this moment, you have had everything that you *needed* (once gain, emphasizing need rather than want): a womb in which the cells of your body multiplied and grew, caregivers to raise you, a nervous system that was capable of learning language, movement and other complex tasks, and the inner resources to succeed at school, work and human relations.

However, let's leave alone the factual accuracy of whether or not you have everything that you need and play pretend for a moment: What if that were actually true? How would that make you feel? What kind of person would you be if you truly believed that you have everything that you need? And what kind of people would you draw into your life if you were that person? *Start there.* In the chapter on beliefs, we will delve deeper into how beliefs empower you and bring you more of what you want.

Chapter 2. Who You Really Are

Right now, as you are sitting there, reading this sentence, a number of answers may come to mind to the question, "Who are you really?" These answers may have to do with various aspects of your supposed identity: your age, for example. Where you were raised. Where you went to school. Your employment. Your preferences in clothing, food, leisure and travel. Your endearing quirks. That cute little dimple you get every time you smile. Your vivacious spirit.

These are all aspects of who you are, but they are not *you*. No single characteristic makes up who you are, and most of them are mutable in any case. Jobs change, habits come and go, temperaments evolve. So what is that stable, immutable part of you which will always be you, your *self*?

The concept of no-self

Buddhist philosophy argues that there is no such thing as a fixed self. Right now, you just took a breath, and trillions of oxygen molecules came from the outside and exchanged with the carbon dioxide in your blood. Billions of blood cells moved around to nourish your body. You just read that last sentence, which means that millions of your neurons fired to see, process and make sense of these words on a page. As a result, you are not exactly the same as you were five seconds ago – *you have changed*. Perhaps not in a way obvious to the naked eye, but in a very real sense, you are different than you were a moment ago.

The ancient Greek philosopher Heraclitus once said that you never bathe in the same river twice, because it's never the same river and it's never the same you. If you were to look at a river, close your eyes, and open them again a few seconds later, every water molecule will have moved, the banks will have rearranged themselves by a little bit, and it will effectively be a brand new river.

You, too, are like a river. There is no fixed version of you. There is no self. The Buddhists call this concept *anatta*, or no-self. In fact, they say that nothing in the world has a fixed self; everything is in flux. Including you.

You may find this concept of no-self distressing: "Oh no! I don't really exist! What am I to do?" Or you may find it a purely philosophical, not terribly practical exercise: "Well, clearly I'm here, so there is some kind of self. What's your point?"

Let me offer another way to look at no-self: as a concept that can be both useful and liberating. Since this book is about dating, let's think about it in a dating context. What would happen if no-self were true?

Well, you wouldn't be afraid of rejection. And you wouldn't be concerned about what others thought or said of you, since there is no you! As a result, you would be willing to approach and speak to any man you fancied. This would vastly increase the range of men you'd be able to date.

Since there's no fixed self to hurt, you'd be less afraid of getting hurt in a relationship and more focused on the enrichment you can derive from the connection. When you do end up dating a man, you would be less likely to feel insulted or slighted by any of his actions, since you can't take any of it personally. Your ego would not get in the way of a good connection. And when the time comes to part, you'd be less likely to feel hurt, rejected or abandoned, since there's no self to be hurt, rejected or abandoned.

Suddenly, this no-self idea seems really handy. Is it really true? Who knows. Can it enrich your life? Absolutely.

For better or for worse, the concept of no-self is easy to grasp but challenging to implement. If we have conditioned ourselves for decades to have an ego and serve it, then we are probably not going to get rid of that tendency overnight. Buddhist monks spend entire lifetimes meditating in monasteries to get to *anatta*. Since that kind of commitment may exceed your available time and patience, here are some practical ways to bring more *anatta* into your life:

1) Meditation. You don't have to spend years in a monastery to derive benefit from meditation. As little as three 15-minute sessions a week is enough to start significant impact on your life.

This reminds me of an old Zen story about a student who comes to his teacher and asks earnestly, "O master, how can I achieve enlightenment?" The teacher says, "Go in that room and meditate about a cow. Just think about that cow with unwavering attention."

So the student goes in the room, and meditates. He doesn't come out all day. And then the next day. And the next. By the third day, the master gets worried, so he asks the student, "Aren't you going to come out?"

And the student replies, "I would, but my horns won't fit through the doorway."

You tend to get more of what you focus on, to the point that you may even *become* what you focus on. So if you concentrate on the idea of no-self diligently, it's bound to take a hold on your consciousness.

Here's a meditation my students have found useful for getting the idea of no-self anchored in their minds. An audio recording of this meditation is **included with this book**. You can find it at www.taoofdating.com/goddess.

Exercise 3. The Galactic Consciousness Meditation

Imagine that you have become very, very small. You are so small that you are the size of a molecule of air. Now imagine that you are in outer space, with nothing around you but the stars and the galaxies. You see them all in their vastness, glory and beauty. Some are so far away that they just look like a ring or disc in the distance. Some are close, and you can appreciate that there are 100 billion stars in a given galaxy, all of different sizes, luminosities, shapes. They are all beautiful, all incredibly vast, unimaginably full of light and energy.

In the corner of one such galaxy, you can discern a tiny blue marble. You start to move towards it, and for a long, long time, there's hardly anything in your way – the occasional bit of cosmic dust, but otherwise the vacuum of space. You get closer and start to discern features of the globe – oceans, continents, swirls of cloud. Eventually, you

---

get close enough to approach the Earth's atmosphere. You encounter molecules of air – just a few at a time at first, then more and more of them. You zip past them, getting closer to the Earth's surface. Gradually you are engulfed by molecules of air. You are swimming in them.

As you approach the Earth's surface, you see a figure who has a striking resemblance to someone you know. Actually it's you, and you get closer and closer to the surface of your own skin. And as you pass through your own skin, you become aware that the density of molecules around you goes up. Remember that you're the size of a single molecule, so as you travel through your own body, you notice its utter vastness – the billions of molecules that make up each cell, the trillions of cells that make up the whole organism. It's as if the body itself is like a galaxy, these countless elements working together to create a living, magnificent being.

You spend some time inside your own body, and then exit out of it into the atmosphere again. And then, you travel past the skin of another person, into another body that's just as vast, just as awe-inspiring as the last one. You travel to another body, and another, and another, noticing all the ways in which they are similar to one another while maintaining their individuality, just like those galaxies you were looking at from outer space. And now you're moving faster and faster, journeying through body after body, and you start to see each cell as a star inside that galaxy. You travel through the bodies of animals, of plants, of every living being, and see them all as they truly are, as expressions of one essence, one truth. As you do that, you eventually return to your own body, and expand and expand, until you inhabit it fully. You are now that galaxy, and you now appreciate the vastness of you, and the kinship you have with everything else in the world. Feel that kinship now, as you bow your head in reverence to your own magnificence, and the magnificence of all of creation.

Another simple technique I like is the *hong-sau meditation*. Sit down with your back upright and your hands on your lap, palms upturned. Now close your eyes and focus on the space between your eyebrows, the 'third-eye center'. Now with each inhalation, say to yourself the sacred Sanskrit syllable *hong*; with each exhalation, silently say *sau* (pronounced like 'saw')[3]. All the while, maintain your concentration on the space between your eyebrows, or third-eye center. You can make this your daily meditation practice, starting at 15 minutes a day and building from there.

2) Do yoga. I think of yoga as a moving meditation. The more vigorous the practice, the better. Why? Because you'll be so busy breathing, holding and balancing, you'll have little mental space left for such trivial matters as the ego.

Once again, the key is to have a regular practice. The more you bathe yourself in this pond, the more of the old notion of self you'll wash away. Practice at least twice a week if you want to see any appreciable results. Three or more times a week and you will notice some serious progress.

3) Use the Reminder Technique. You may have heard of the holy month of Ramadhan in Muslim cultures where everyone fasts for a month. One of the requirements for your fast to be acceptable is to keep your thoughts and deeds pure in addition to refraining from eating and drinking. That gnawing hunger you experience in the pit of your belly is a reminder to be a better kind of person all day long. And the idea is that, after a whole month of that, you stand a real chance of behaving differently the other eleven months of the year, too.

------

[3] The syllables *hong* and *sau* have no translation; just use them as sacred sounds to focus the mind.

You can do a similar version of that for the idea of no-self. An elastic wristband, a ring, an ink mark on your right thumb – anything can serve as your reminder to live the concept of no-self during the day. Use this reminder several weeks in a row, and the idea may just stick.

4) *Experience flow.* Psychologist Mihaly Czikszentmihaly (pronounced 'cheeks sent me high') talks about *flow* – that optimal state in which the task is matched to the ability. You're stretching yourself just a little bit, so the task is challenging (as opposed to boring) without being frustrating.

All of us have experienced flow at some point or another. For a pianist, it could be the performance of a Brahms prelude. For a rower, it could be that time when the whole crew works together as a unit and the boat 'swings'. For a surfer, it could be paddling at just the right speed to catch and surf a perfect wave.

Whatever flow is, you've got to find it for you. And start doing that thing more and more. Why? Because when you're in flow, you *are* the action. Ego dissolves, and there is no more you – there is only do. So think back to all those times when you were in flow, and seek out those activities again. You may be surprised to find yourself revisiting something you haven't done in a long time which you still find strangely gratifying.

5) *Travel.* Of all of the methods listed above, this may very well be the most potent. Much of what you consider your fixed identity is anchored into your environment: your dwelling, your workplace, the streets you usually drive, the supermarket you usually shop at, the drink you usually order, the people you usually hang out with, the clothes you usually wear.

Remove all those hooks, and a new version of you (or no-you) has a chance to emerge. The more removed the locale from your everyday experience, the more likely you are to let go of the fixed notion of self.

So go hang out with some Galapagos turtles, Peruvian shamans, African springboks, and Mongolian herdsmen. Then write back and tell me how it went.

There's one method that's guaranteed not to give you any results at all, and that's doing what you have been doing all along. Nothing changes if nothing changes. This book is about getting results by *taking action*. No action, no results. You've taken one big step towards getting results by purchasing this book and reading this far. If you really want to test the idea of no-self and reap its benefits in your life, commit to doing at least two of the above steps now. You'll be glad you did.

Who you really are

We've talked about how you are not some static entity known as the self. Let's say you agree with that. So what *are* you then?

We've got a lot of options here, so let's try this one on for size: you are a conduit for abundance in the universe. To say that you are a conduit means that abundance is already present in the universe; you are merely the instrument it passes through. Since you are the conduit, you do not get to own any of the abundance; you are just the pipeline.

Expanding on that idea, you are also a conduit for right action, or *te*. *Te* is the implementation aspect of the Tao. Taoism is far from being a passive philosophy. It is about taking right action so in consonance with the Tao, so in tune with the natural way of things, that it *seems* effortless, the way water flows downstream. When you become one with the flow of the Tao, your actions take on a lightness, grace and effectiveness that they wouldn't have when they were emanating from the ego. You abolish struggle.

Another idea to ponder has roots in every ancient spiritual system. In the Hindu tradition, it is called *advaita*, which is Sanskrit for non-duality. It simply means that there is a ground of being, a basic essence from which all beings in the universe arise. Plainly stated, it is about how we are all cut from the same fabric.

Rationally, this is easy to grasp: we're all made of the same molecules and atoms that make up the rest of the universe. The chair you're sitting on, the air you're breathing, the clothes you're wearing are all made of the same molecules of carbon, oxygen, nitrogen, hydrogen, etc. By extension, you can imagine that there is also a spiritual essence that makes up all beings and the whole of the universe. And you are made of that.

If this seems like an abstract concept to you right now, don't worry. Monks spend years meditating on this so they can fully grasp their oneness with the universe at a visceral level. As long as you are interested in grasping this concept and applying it to your life, you will.

Perhaps some day you'll start a regular meditation practice (if you don't already have one) and really feel the meaning of *advaita* in your bones. In the meantime, the passage below from an ancient Hindu text is one of the best I have encountered in explaining how all beings are made of the same essence. In it, King Aruni is explaining the concept of non-duality to his son Svetaketu, who has just returned from his long studies:

> *The bees, my dear son, prepare honey by gathering the nectar of different trees and reducing that nectar to a unity. So that the nectar from each different tree is not able to differentiate: "I am*

the nectar of this tree" and "I am the nectar of that tree." In exactly the same way, my son, when all creatures merge into reality, they are not aware that "We are merging into reality." No matter what they are in this world – whether they are a tiger, a lion, a wolf, a boar, a worm, a moth, a gnat, or a mosquito – they all merge into that reality. That finest essence here is the self of the whole world. That is reality; that is the self. And thou art that.

— Chandogya Upanishad, *translated by* R. *Hume, p. 264*

Embracing The Goddess

Western society has a pervasive habit of self-diminishment. As children, we are told that pride is the deadliest of the seven mortal sins. Hubris brought Achilles down, and if we're not careful, it will surely bring us down, too. Thus, many of us spend our lives overcompensating for this fear of egotism. We politely deflect compliments, try our best not to seem too smart, too pretty, too stylish. We compete in self-deprecation contests to see who can put herself down the most.

Now I'm not quite sure how you benefit from hiding your light under a bushel. How does playing small and feeling small enrich the world around you? In fact, diminishing your gifts is a selfish act since you're depriving all those around you of your light. And as a woman, the world needs your light now more than ever.

There is no more eloquent expression of this idea than in Marianne Williamson's *Return to Love*:

Our greatest fear is not that we are inadequate. Our greatest fear is that we are powerful beyond measure. It is our light, not our darkness that most frightens us. We ask ourselves, who am I to be brilliant, fabulous, gorgeous, talented? Actually, who are you not to be? You are a child of God. Your playing small doesn't serve the world. There's nothing enlightened about shrinking so that other people won't feel insecure around you. We were born to make manifest the glory of God that's within us. It's not just in some of us. It's in everyone. And as we let our own light shine, we automatically give other people permission to do the same. As we are liberated from our own fears, our presence automatically liberates others.

So I would like to propose an alternative to this regime of self-diminishment: the embracing of the Goddess within. In many Eastern spiritual traditions, especially the various forms of Tantra, we are all manifestations of divine energy. Thus, as a woman, you are the incarnation of the divine in female human form.

At some point before, you may have heard the idea that you contain the Goddess within you. You may have even found it interesting and appealing if somewhat abstract, not certain how it would apply to your life.

I'd like to bring to your attention that, far from being an abstraction, the idea of embodying the Goddess is an eminently practical one, with immediate, life-changing consequences. Because Goddess status is not something that you apply for or wait to receive when you are worthy. The Goddess is already within you, waiting to emerge. You just have to let it. In her excellent book *A Woman's Worth* (which I highly recommend if you haven't read it already), Williamson says:

We think of ourselves as flesh and bone, resumes and relationships, clothes and cosmetics. The truth of who we are, why we're here and where we're going is far more spectacular than any of these worldly things indicate. We are God's precious vessels and we are always pregnant with his possibilities.

The way to allow the Goddess to emerge is simple: *act as if you already are her.* If the Goddess represents infinite kindness, then you act with infinite kindness. If the Goddess is grace, then you behave graciously. If the Goddess is nurturance, then you nurture those around you. If the Goddess is strength, then you are strong and give strength to those around you. If the Goddess is radiance, then you shine your light wherever you go.

Exercise 4. Embodying the Goddess

What does the word *goddess* mean to you? Take a few minutes to write down what comes to your mind as you complete this sentence: "To be the Goddess is to be the embodiment of ..." Here are some ideas to get you started: wisdom, beauty, grace, joy, sensuality, nurturance, passion, kindness, forgiveness, strength, radiance.

Now that you have your list, take a moment to imagine what it would be like if you were to embody those characteristics. What would you look like? How would you move differently? What would it feel like in your body? Imagine a few situations you were in this week, and notice how you would handle them differently if you were embodying the Goddess. What would you say? How would you act? Imagine some scenarios in the future – at home, at work, or in a social setting. What do you notice about yourself?

Finally, imagine yourself interacting with a man you're interested in – perhaps a former or future companion. What is the quality of the connection? How does the relationship unfold differently from before?

If you are not yet completely comfortable with the idea that you are the Goddess, that's okay. Do the exercise anyway. Do it again. And again. Eventually, it will feel right.

And sooner than you think, it takes hold in your consciousness.

This is not about egotism. It's not about being better than anyone else. It's simply about exercising the choice to become who you already are. Once again in *A Woman's Worth*, Williamson says: "At every moment, a woman makes a choice: between the state of the queen and the state of the slavegirl." Embodying your true power as Queen and Goddess is a choice – one you can make right now.

When you are the queen, the Goddess, then the right kind of men – the Warriors, the Kings – will naturally gravitate towards you. The slavegirl will also attract men, but she's much more likely to attract the wrong kind. When you flourish into the most glorious, radiant, version of you, people will take notice – especially the good men. But that is merely a side benefit. Much more important is that you will feel alive and empowered, which is its own reward:

> *When a woman has owned her passionate nature, allowing love to flood her heart, her thoughts grow wild and fierce and beautiful... When a woman conceives her true self, a miracle occurs and life around her begins again.*
>
> – *Marianne Williamson*, A Woman's Worth

Your shortcut to divinity

If I were to pick one and only one quality that would bring out your goddess nature and make you irresistible to men, it would have to be *radiance*. It encompasses earthly aspects: radiant health, glowing skin, radiant smile. It encompasses metaphysical aspects as well: radiating positive energy, shining the light of the divine.

That's nice, you say, but how do you *do* that? Well, if I told you that doing one simple practice would make you irresistibly radiant to almost any man, and remove every woman as competition, would you do it? Think about that for a second.

What if I told you that this practice would require all of your courage and a complete re-thinking of who you are? Would you still do it?

The practice is simple, and it encompasses nearly everything we discussed in Exercise 4. It is called *devotion* (which may mean something different than what you think). If you are able to convey complete and utter devotion to a man, he will feel so energized, so elevated, so manly that he will have absolutely nowhere to go but to you. You will be irresistible. We will discuss devotion and how to practice it in an empowering context in Chapter 10 when we talk about attraction.

Chapter 3. Yin and Yang

Taoist philosophy talks about how universal energy has two aspects to it: feminine *yin* energy and masculine *yang* energy. They are not opposite to one another as much as they are complementary. Every coin has two sides, and every mountain casts a shadow. In the same way that the two sides of a coin form a unit, so do yin and yang. In Chapter 2 of the *Tao Te Ching*, Lao Tzu says:

> *Being and non-being create each other.*
> *Difficult and easy support each other.*
> *Long and short define each other.*
> *High and low depend on each other.*
> *Before and after follow each other.*

Everything in the universe has both yin and yang aspects to it. The *taijitu* symbol of Taoism – the circle with the black area holding a dot of white, and a white area holding a dot of black – illustrates this concept: there is a little bit of yang (white) in the middle of the yin (black), and a little bit of yin in the field of yang.

In a similar fashion, women hold both masculine and feminine energy within them (as do men). There is a physiological parallel to this as well. Men's primary sex hormone is testosterone, with estrogen secondary. Women's primary sex hormone is estrogen, with testosterone as secondary.

Feminine yin energy encompasses receptivity, generativity, and yielding. In Taoist philosophy, this is symbolized by water, the ocean or earth. Masculine yang energy is about motion, action and giving; fire is its Taoist symbol.

In the language of modern psychological research, feminine functions are known as *expressivity* while masculine ones are *instrumentality*. We will use these terms interchangeably. In *A Woman's Worth*, Williamson has a lucid description of masculine and feminine and the difference between them: "The masculine is active, the feminine passive; the masculine is dynamic, the feminine magnetic. The masculine *does* while the feminine *is*."

Regardless of which terminology you prefer, the yin/yang idea is a powerful one, clarifying many aspects of romance while empowering you in the process. For example, we all express different amounts of yin and yang depending on our station in life, time of year, career situation, even time of day. You may spend your days as a business owner, corporate consultant, high-powered attorney or President of the United States. During these times, you are predominantly utilizing your yang aspect: leading, directing, deciding. Yet you may also be a mother, and when you return home, you switch to the more feeling yin aspect of your energy when dealing with your children.

Balancing yin and yang in partnerships

Although as a woman, your predominant tone is yin, masculine and feminine energies are fluid. Like the tides, yin and yang ebb and rise depending on position and time. While men are predominantly yang, some men have a strong yin energy.

In the context of a relationship, the point to keep in mind is not the absolute value of someone's energy, but rather to look for energy *complementarity* between partners. Even in a same-sex relationship, one partner will end up being more yin, the other more yang. As in positive and negative charge, or north and south poles of a magnet, *polarity* is the basis of bringing things together. A connection between yin and yang has polarity, whereas yin-yin and yang-yang have none.

In psychological terminology, a person with more instrumentality is best partnered up with someone who has more expressivity. Both partners can also be *androgynous*, meaning that they embody both instrumentality and expressivity, yang and yin. In fact, research shows that people who demonstrate both yin and yang energies are easier to get along with.

Let us illustrate these concepts with an example. Jennifer was a successful attorney who saw her marriage of five years coming to an end. When I asked her what precipitated the break, she expressed that her husband wasn't strong enough (actual wording: "He was too wimpy"). One way of interpreting this is that he wasn't expressing enough yang, resulting in a yin-yang imbalance and a loss of polarity. This may have been because she was bringing home a lot of the leading, directive yang energy that her job required. So now, the amount of yang energy the man used to have at the beginning of the relationship – which was probably sufficient when they first got married – was insufficient. This led to a flattening of their relationship and the loss of the spark of passion, which needs the flow of energy between opposite poles.

One way to improve this relationship is to restore the yin-yang polarity. This can happen in several ways: the man steps up his yang; the woman embraces more of her yin, feminine aspect; or some mixture of the two. If the man is plenty masculine already, then the first solution will most likely result in a clash of yang energies, which is a bit like two partners on the dance floor both trying to lead. The other solution is for one of the partners to yield, embracing yin.

It's important to remember that *yielding is not the same as submission or losing*. Quite the opposite: when one dance partner allows the other to lead, both end up having a lot more fun. And it's not a competition in any case: it's a partnership. It's a win-win situation. In tantric philosophy, the feminine finds its ultimate fulfillment in yielding and surrender. Whether or not that resonates with you, there are times when it is good to lead, and times when it is good to follow. Once again, Chapter 29 of the *Tao Te Ching*:

There is a time for being ahead,
A time for being behind;
A time for being in motion,
A time for being at rest;
A time for being vigorous,
A time for being exhausted;
A time for being safe,
A time for being in danger.

The dilemma of the career-oriented woman

If you are reading this book, you are probably a well-educated, career-oriented woman. That's because I wrote this book specifically with you in mind. Being a talented, driven and successful woman creates unique challenges in the dating domain.

There's a popular conception of how for thousands of years, perhaps even until the 1950s, gender roles roughly mirrored the yin-yang duality. Men were engaged in instrumental functions – hunting or working outside the home – while women stayed at home and took care of the household. Each party appreciated what the other brought to the table, literally and figuratively. Men appreciated the nurturing function of women and their role in raising children, and women were grateful for their men going out and bringing back home a hunk of woolly mammoth for dinner.

That was a long time ago. Many more women now have the choice to pursue an education and career instead of taking on the traditional gender role of staying at home and raising children. As a result, there are many women who are tremendously successful in the traditionally male-dominated workforce. According to Taoist philosophy, this is expected, since we all have both yin and yang energy within us.

Women are just as capable of turning on their yang energy and being driven, competitive, powerful leaders as men are of turning on their expressive yin energy and crying over the death of a pet.

However, there is a side effect to this. Whenever anyone spends most of her time and energy on a certain pursuit, then she will come to *identify* herself more and more with that pursuit (remember the parable of meditating on a cow). In other words, it becomes challenging to turn off the work mentality when it takes up so much of your existence. It reminds me of the old medical school parties, when the spouses of the surgeons would complain that the husband (or wife) was too domineering, running the household as if it were an operating room and he (or she) the undisputed ruler. The surgeons couldn't turn off the surgeon at home, annoying everyone around them and straining their relationships.

Hence, the dilemma of the modern woman. The strength and leadership that a career-oriented woman exhibit are tremendously appealing qualities to almost all educated men I know. However, unless they are expressed in the context of a woman's feminine energies, they are more likely to evoke feelings of respect and admiration rather than attraction.

Men are generally not attracted to women because of how well they emulate male qualities. Men are attracted to your *femininity*. Think of it this way: how attractive would you find a man with a lot of feminine energy? Men are likely to react the same way towards a woman with a lot of masculine energy. And embracing your femininity is not an abdication of your power; rather, it is the ultimate *acceptance* of your power.

So if you express your masculine energies at home in the same way you do at work, you are likely to be respected and admired (and perhaps a little feared), but perhaps not cherished. In *A Woman's Worth*, Williamson calls this the Amazon neurosis, "the woman who achieves at the expense of her tender places."

There is another way, of course. If you wish to be cherished, celebrated *and* incredibly attractive to men, you may wish to relinquish some of the yang when you're at home and embrace the full power of the feminine. As Williamson put it, "In intimate relationships with men, I want to major in feminine and minor in masculine."

Yin and yang in a relationship

I have noticed that many women in relationships feel that it is their job to steer its course and provide most of the fuel to propel it. She will be the one to initiate serious talks about where the relationship is headed and to give of her time and energy to keep the relationship going. However, from a yin-yang perspective, leading and giving are *masculine* functions. Even though there is a tendency to think that giving is a feminine function, at its essence it's a masculine one. The feminine is the *receptive*.

Of course, in any true partnership, both parties are engaged in giving *and* taking, which in its highest form manifests as sharing. However, it's important to keep in mind that if you take over the masculine function of giving, then it leaves no room for the man to do that.

Therefore one way to think about relationships is in terms of depth and direction. The depth is a function of yin; the direction is a function of yang. And so, roughly speaking, the masculine will be in charge of the direction of the relationship, while the feminine will be responsible for its depth.

Although we will talk more about what to do once you are in a relationship, keep in mind that this book is mostly about dating, not relationships. Once you've successfully navigated the waters of dating to arrive at a relationship, you may wish to seek out some of the resources featured at the end of the book (e.g. the works of professor of psychology John Gottman).

Chapter 4. What You Really Want

What do you want from your dating life? Most people don't have a concrete answer to this question. And the people who *think* they know what they want sometimes end up getting it, only to realize it's not quite what they expected (affective forecasting again).

As we discussed early in the book, what we want from a relationship (and almost everything else in life) are fulfilling feelings. Once you think of it that way, you realize that you're not looking for a particular kind of person, of a certain height or hair color or socioeconomic status, but rather the feelings that person evokes in you.

You also realize that fulfillment is more of an internal phenomenon than an external one, depending on yourself more than anything. It's not about what your parents or friends think. It's not about how strangers look at the two of you together. It's about how your values are fulfilled on the inside.

At any point in life, what you think you want may vary. And often what we think we want doesn't really fulfill us when we get it. As stated earlier, we're quite bad at affective forecasting, always overestimating how much things will make us happy (or unhappy) in the long term. However, your values tend to remain constant. That's because values are deep, unconscious motivators that give the general sense of purpose and direction to your life. Although values are the strongest drivers of our overall behavior, we often don't know about them until they are violated, much like how we notice the stomach only when we have a stomach ache.

There are two more ways of figuring out what your values are besides having them violated. One is by noticing events that fulfill them, and the other is through conscious inner exploration. The next exercise will get you started on that exploration. For further resources on figuring out your values, I recommend the book *NLP: The New Technology of Achievement*, which has a series of drills in the chapter entitled 'Discovering Your Mission,' from which the following list of values was adapted.

Exercise 5. Empower yourself by figuring out your core values

What are your values in life? From the list below, pick ten values that you feel are most important to you. If there's a value that is important to you that you do not see on the list, add it on.

Write down your ten values. Now, if you could have one and only one of these, which one would it be? Mark it "1." Now, from the remaining nine values, if you could have one and just one, which one would it be? Mark it "2." Continue this process until you have your top 5 values.

---

autonomy	beauty	caring	challenge
courage	creativity	dignity	elegance
excellence	excitement	fairness	freedom
fulfillment	fun	grace	happiness
abundance	power	kindness	respect
family	humility	education	bliss
harmony	helping	honesty	humor
innovation	joy	justice	learning
love	mastery	order	perseverance
playfulness	revolution	safety	security
self-actualization	self-reliance	service	simplicity
problem-solving	creating change	synergy	truth
uniqueness	vitality	wisdom	zest

Let's revisit the question from the beginning of the chapter. What do you want from your dating life? The answer is you want from your dating life the same things you want from your life in general. Values affect all areas of your life, so your overall values for life tend to be the same ones as your values for relationships. Once you know what your values are, you can decide how you'd like to fulfill them.

It's best to fulfill your values in a way that creates the least amount of conflict amongst your top values. Let's say one of your values is adventure. You can experience that in the context of having one adventure with several men, or several adventures with one man. If another one of your values is variety, then you will probably choose the former option. If one of your values is stability, then perhaps you will choose the latter option.

You now have an internal compass for knowing when a given relationship is aligned with your values. If your values are being matched, the relationship will naturally flourish. If not, the relationship will falter and you will want to move on.

What you have to offer

Would you date yourself? I'm not asking a frivolous question. For a moment, take the perspective of a man who is actually interested in you. Perhaps you have even been on a couple of dates together. Now, ask yourself these questions: "What draws me to this woman? Why do I want to see her again?" Take a look at the inventory of values that you came up with in the previous exercise (and if you didn't do the exercise, go back and do it – the rest of the book hinges upon that information). How many of those would you be able to fulfill in a relationship with a man?

Exercise 6. Walking the walk
Determine how many of the values you came up with in Exercise 5 are ones you can actually provide in a relationship.

It's very important to be honest with yourself in this exercise. No one is looking over your shoulder, and all of this information is for your benefit alone, so it is to your great advantage to provide the most accurate information possible.

Now look at that list of values again. If you feel that you can provide many of those values in a relationship, great. You need not possess *all* of them, since yin-yang dynamics is about complementarity, too. For example, you can appreciate humor in your man without being a stand-up comic yourself. But if you're missing most of the values that you demand in a partner, perhaps you have some work to do in those departments.

For example, let's say *spontaneity* and *honesty* are two values that you cherish in a relationship, yet you tend to shy away from new activities, or be very secretive about your thoughts and feelings. Since this is clearly not compatible with your stated values of spontaneity and honesty, you must either change your behavior to become consistent with your values, or change your values to become consistent with your behavior. To demand certain standards from your partners, it's a good idea to meet them yourself first.

Exercise 7. Take stock of your relationship assets
Write down everything about you that is interesting and attractive. What reasons would a man have to see you again, or to stay with you in a relationship?

This exercise is an assessment of what you offer in a relationship. Are you funny? Exceptionally generous and kind? A great cook? Do you provide witty conversation? Can you stimulate his mind? His body? Do you have exceptional sexual expertise? Do you have an infectious sense of adventure and wonder? Write down every reason that a man would want to spend time with you, from the most trivial to the most important.

Having done that, let's take a brutally honest look at this list to find out which of the items would actually *matter* to a man. For example, you may have exceptionally good taste in upholstery, or have shoes to fit any and every occasion. But will he necessarily care about that? You want to assess what *he* (not your girlfriends) will see as an asset.

But how do you make this assessment? What do men really want? The broad answer to that is that men (and women) seek things that makes them feel good. Your mastery of the subtleties of women's shoes is probably not one of those things. Your massage skill, on the other hand, is a much better bet.

Yin, yang and three stages of relationship

As we discussed in Chapter 3, the principle of polarity governs attraction in the universe. Positive charge is attracted to negative charge, whereas like charges repel one another. The north pole of a magnet attracts the south pole. And so it is with masculine and feminine. For there to be a spark, a flow of energy between two entities, there needs to be polarity. This seems to be particularly true in relationships between men and women.

And so masculine and feminine are two manifestations of the universal life principle. Everyone possesses elements of both masculine and feminine energy. Men tend to have more masculine energy, or *yang* according to Taoist tradition, and women tend to have more feminine energy, or *yin*. What's important to remember is that for there to be a flow of energy and vitality within a relationship, there needs to be polarity, regardless of which party has more masculine or feminine energy.

Let's examine this in the context of male-female relationships. I find David Deida's simple but powerful way of describing relationships through three stages useful as a general framework.

The first stage relationship is between a macho jerk and a dependent, submissive woman. The man is strong but not terribly considerate and carries a lot of masculine energy. He has a lot of spine, but no heart. The woman, on the other hand, will do anything to get even a little bit of love. She has a lot of feminine energy. She has a lot of heart, but not much spine. Sure, there is plenty of polarity in this relationship, but there's much left to be desired. We call this the codependence stage, and room for growth within this kind of relationship is limited at best.

The second stage relationship is between the sensitive man and the independent woman. This is a man who realizes that women want a guy who listens, who is in touch with his feelings, who has an open heart. So he has taken it upon himself to bring more feminine yin energy into his life. The woman in this kind of relationship is strong and independent. Typically, she has a job with a lot of responsibility. She can take care of herself financially and doesn't really need a man. As such, she has brought a fair amount of masculine yang energy on board.

This is the independence stage. Although this kind of relationship is a progression from the first, much of the polarity is lost in the feminizing of the man and the masculinizing of the woman. Such relationships tend to fall flat after a while, and may very well be part of the reason behind the high divorce rates nowadays. The man in this kind of relationship has a lot more heart than the first-stage fellow; however, in the process, he has lost much of his spine.

The third stage relationship is between the man as a spiritual warrior and the woman as a fully-realized goddess. Here, the man is able and willing to take the woman deeper into her feminine essence than she could by herself. And the woman, in turn, is able to guide the man deeper into his life's purpose than he could by himself. I call this the stage of mutual flourishing. The man in this kind of relationship has both heart and spine, both compassion and unwavering purpose. He is the combination of the best elements of the man from the Stage 1 and Stage 2 relationships. Notice also that in this stage, compared to Stage 1, both the man and the woman are adept at taking on the complementary energy (yin for men, yang for women) while the guy majors in masculine and the girl majors in feminine.

	Man	**Woman**
Stage 1: Co-dependent	all spine, no heart	no spine, all heart
Stage 2: Independent	less spine, more heart	more spine, less heart
Stage 3: Mutual Flourishing	both spine and heart	both spine and heart

The kind of guy you would want

Now that we've discussed the types of relationships that are possible with a man, it's easier to create a picture of the kind of man who would fit in that picture. As we said before, you're much more likely to find something if you have a good idea of what you're looking for. Throughout this book, we're going to talk about a prototype of a man with whom you're most likely to have a fulfilling relationship. He's the fellow from the Third Stage relationship we described above – the spiritual warrior, the man with both compassion *and* purpose, heart *and* spine. For short, henceforth I will call him the *Good Guy*, and we shall spend some time describing him in detail during the course of this book – things that will aid you in spotting him and inviting him into your life.

Now as you are sitting somewhere and reading this book, my dear reader, I don't really know you that well. However, I assume that if you've taken it upon yourself to pick up this book, you are interested in a fulfilling relationship. Fulfillment comes in many shapes and sizes, and the *Tao of Dating* is about giving you the tools to find that fulfillment, regardless of your starting point. Roughly speaking, we'll categorize relationships into three categories by duration – short, medium and long-term – and see how each guy fits in. Regardless of what constitutes your fulfillment, it helps if you enter into each kind of relationship consciously, knowing roughly what to expect.

Short-term relationships (also known as 'flings'). This is the kind of relationship you enter without expecting it to last long. It could be anything from an evening's encounter to a one-week vacation romance to a summer-long fling. The distinction here is your mindset: you are entering this relationship with few expectations as to long-term potential.

For this kind of relationship, any of the three kinds of men will probably do. However, there are ramifications. The first-stage guy, masculine but not very heart-centered, is the one you're most likely to have fun with while managing a clean break at the end. We'll call him Biff. The second-stage guy – the sensitive guy, whom we will dub Lance – is the one most likely to be hurt at the end. He'll probably try to keep in touch, calling and writing to tell you how much he misses you and how much you mean to him. This could be sweet but annoying at the same time. The third-stage guy – both strong and compassionate, whom we will call Victor – can handle whatever happens just fine. However, *you* will be more likely to be hurt at the end, realizing how much he meant to you and wanting more from him than he may be able to offer.

Medium-term relationships (also known as 'serious relationship' or 'boyfriend'). There comes a time when you want to be with a man for the long term, but not necessarily forever. You're ready for a lease, but maybe not a full purchase – a boyfriend, but not a husband. You're not necessarily entering the relationship thinking, "Well, this is going to last a few months and then I'll be moving along," but in effect that's what it is.

Starting with this kind of relationship, it's best to toss out the Stage 1 guy *completely*. Biff is at best a dessert, enjoyed sparingly; he is *never* a main course. If you substitute dessert for real, nutritious food on a regular basis, you *will* be unhappy and unhealthy, which is precisely the effect of having a Biff in your life long-term.

The Stage 2 guy – Lance – is fine for this kind of relationship. You have (and will have) many joyous, fulfilling relationships with Lance. Just be aware that the full flourishing of you will probably not occur with a Lance, and so turning him into a marriage prospect, as sensible as it may seem at the moment, is likely to be a formula for long-term disappointment. And we're all about enlightened self-interest here, which has your *long-term* fulfillment in mind. He just may not be ready for you – ever.

Finally, there's Victor, the Stage 3 guy. He would be great for this kind of relationship (or any kind, really). The only issue is that if you're not on the market for marriage, you may not be ready for *him*. Reverse disappointment is still disappointment, and teasing yourself with this amazing guy with whom you can't stay (for whatever reason) is something to consider.

Long-term relationships (also known as 'marriage' or 'life partnership'). For this kind of relationship, I can only recommend the Stage 3 man. You are long done with Biff, you can handle Lance fine but he can't handle you, and now you're ready for the real thing. Although there are probably more Lances and Biffs than Victors, there are are still plenty of Victors out there, so keep an eye out for them. The good news is that many Lances have the capacity to turn into Victors, especially when they are in relationship with a fully-realized goddess (that would be you). If anything has the power to transform, it is love, so take heart.

Chapter 5. Understanding Men, Understanding Yourself

The purpose of this chapter is to give you some general insight into men's dating behavior. After reading it, you may still not be able to predict guy behavior, but you'll have an outside chance of understanding it instead of being baffled by it.

Note that there are as many different types of men as there are males inhabiting this planet – about 3.2 billion of them so far. Attempting to boil down this exceptionally diverse cohort into a handful of tidy generalizations would be an oversimplification that does disservice to both you and the men. As Voltaire once said, "All generalizations are false, including this one." It's still best to examine each male specimen that comes along your way on a case-by-case basis.

At the same time, there are some principles that hold true about male behavior most (but not necessarily all) of the time. To paraphrase Shylock from Shakespeare's *The Merchant of Venice*, if you prick them they will bleed, if you tickle them they will laugh, and if you stand them up for a date they will be seriously bummed out. Men are people, too.

Subsequent to a spate of popular psychology books from the 1990s, the myth that men and women behave so differently as to be from different planets seems to have taken hold in the public imagination. Like most myths, these differences have not been supported by scientific evidence. As far as I can tell, men are from Earth and women are, too, and human beings are much more similar than they are different, regardless of sex. In fact, the behavioral and communicational differences between individual women (and between individual men) will be far greater than the differences between men and women as a group.

That said, there *are* some differences between the way men and women are built. Some of these differences have behavioral ramifications, and entire books have been written on the subject (see Pease & Pease). This book you are reading is about dating, so I will concentrate on what's relevant to that.

What's important here is to be *cognizant* of the differences. This is the first step towards understanding and perhaps tolerating what you may perceive as men's quirks. Remember – if almost all men exhibit a certain behavioral pattern, then it's not just a quirk. It's just the way they are, just part of the Tao. And, as some wise person once said, first seek to understand, then to be understood. So, from an actual guy to you, let's find out how we tick.

Why men are so damn horny

A fair amount of evidence points to men wanting sex and seeking it out far more often than women. During the few hundred thousand years that human beings evolved on the savannah, sexual activity for a woman could potentially result in pregnancy, with its concomitant investment of resources, reduced mobility, and risk of death during childbirth. In comparison, the cost of sexual activity for a male is a few milliliters of semen which he can regenerate in short order. And, should there be a pregnancy, he's not the one who has to carry and raise the child.

A simple way to understand the difference between male and female reproductive strategies is to answer this question for yourself: what is the maximum number of children a man and a woman could have in a year if each had sex with a different person every day? It becomes immediately obvious that, in the genetic lottery, a man stands to gain a lot more from having multiple partners. Hence the difference in sexual behavior.

That said, women are horny, too. A famous diagram of sex drive (see Pease & Pease) shows that men's sex drive peaks in their teens and early twenties, then steadily declines. Women's, on the other hand, rises steadily (always less than that of the men) until the late thirties and early forties, when it surpasses men's sex drive. Perhaps that's where the expression 'dirty thirties' comes from.

Taoist philosophy says that one of the keys to living a good life is to observe the way the world is and then to flow with it, as opposed to trying to shoehorn the world into some notion of how you think it *should* be. These notions manifest in various forms: religion, culture, local custom, family upbringing, fad, trend. My definition of pain is *wishing the world to be different than it is*. So, to avoid pain in your relationships with men, it's good to observe human sexuality and the patterns that have emerged over thousands of years and work *with* them, not against them. You don't have to like the way it is, but you can at least make your peace with it.

> **Pain is wishing the world to be different than it is.**

Making your peace with monogamy (or absence thereof)

Primatologists have measured the ratio of testicle size to body weight in various primates and observed an interesting correlation. Species with a high testicle-to-body-weight ratio, such as chimpanzees and bonobos, tend to be more promiscuous than species with a lower ratio, such as gorillas (who have sex maybe once a year). *Homo sapiens* fits somewhere in between chimps and gorillas, which would predict that we humans would be chiefly monogamous with some excursions outside the pair bond. Studies bear out what literature, history and our own experience hint at being true: both human males and females are inclined to engage in what anthropologists call *extra-pair couplings*, even within the context of a monogamous relationship. Although both genders stray, men do it at a higher rate than women.

Strict monogamy is quite rare in the entire animal kingdom and may not exist at all[4]. And until recently, polygamy seems to have been more common than not. Historically men were involved in aggression and war, and each battle reduced their numbers. This led to a perennial shortage of men, making polygamy an effective survival

---

[4] For a thorough, warm and humorous treatment of this subject, I recommend *The Myth of Monogamy*, by the husband-and-wife team of David Barash and Judith Lipton

strategy for the tribe so the widows were taken care of. Thus it makes sense that one study showed a slight majority of human cultures studied all over the globe to be polygamous in nature.

Men have extra-pair couplings, and so do women. A study conducted in England by zoologist Robin Baker between 1988 and 1996 revealed that the biological fathers of 10% of the population was not whom they expected it to be. So be careful the next time you call someone a bastard, since you may be closer to the truth than you think.

Another study involving women rating the attractiveness of male faces showed an interesting result. The women in the study usually preferred the more feminine-looking male faces except for when they were ovulating. During that time, they had a marked preference for the more masculine-looking faces. This may mean that, depending on time of the month, women pick different sex partners for different purposes: the more nurturing-looking ones for raising the family, and the more rugged-looking ones for sexy genes to pass on to their offspring.

The point of citing these studies and observations isn't to condone or condemn one type of behavior over another. It's simply to tell you that these things happen, have been happening and will continue to happen. If you see these tendencies for what they are without labeling, judging or getting all worked up about them, you'll probably have more peace of mind – and get more of what you want.

So if you come across a handsome, virile, well-to-do fellow that you fancy, be prepared for him not to be a celibate monk. And if you two start dating, it's quite possible that he'll be seeing other women unless he tells you he's not. And if you get married, know that even you yourself may someday have an office fling. These things happen, so know them, expect them, plan for them, and place them in the larger context of your long-term fulfillment. Monogamy need not be completely out of the question. Just know that you don't need to make something relatively uncommon an absolute requirement for your fulfillment.

Know what you're getting yourself into

To put this all in practical terms, if you've started dating a man, it's possible that he will be seeing other women at the same time. Just so there are no surprises for you, assume that until a man has made an explicit promise of sexual exclusivity to you, he will reserve the latitude to be intimate with other women. In the meantime, you are free to date other men, too.

Although you may not be able to tell *him* what to do, you have control over setting *your* boundaries. For health reasons and just to clarify where you stand, it's wise to know whether your date is having sexual relations with other people and decide how comfortable you are with that. A simple, direct question usually gets that information for you, provided it's at the appropriate time. "When was the last time you had sex?" gets to the heart of the matter and is perfectly appropriate if you're already having sex or heading in that direction, especially if you preface it with your genuine concern for health. If that's too direct for you, then "Are you seeing anyone else?" will usually yield the same information.

If you're considering sleeping with a man, you also have a right to know whether he's engaging in safer sex or not. So ask him. Be wary if you get anything but a simple, direct answer back. If you feel that his behavior violates your values or endangers your health, you may wish to look elsewhere. Of course, it goes without saying that you will always engage in safer sex.

Kill the prince

I noticed a curious irony when I was speaking to my friend Heather the other day. I asked her about her weekend date, and she said, "Oh, I had a really great time. This guy was really fun, good-looking, and we were laughing the whole time. After the theater we went to this late night café and talked until 3am." I said, "That's fantastic! When are you going to see him again?" She responded, "Well, I don't know. I'm not sure if there's going to be a second date. I didn't feel that instant chemistry, you know, those butterflies in your stomach, that tingle you get all over your body that says *this guy is the one.*"

Well, that's interesting. Clearly she's had a good time, and yet she's reluctant to follow up. Sometimes this happens because she's had relationships in the past which have started with that 'big spark'. But the irony is that all those relationships that started with intense chemistry and the big spark have ended, leaving her – single. Those men aren't around anymore. Although this does not invalidate those relationships, it does make one wonder if instant chemistry is indeed the prerequisite for a fulfilling long-term relationship.

This leads us to an even bigger irony. I always make a point of asking women in happy relationships – married or not – about how they first met their partners. And before even getting started with the story, many of them say, "You know, the first time I met him I didn't really like him that much." So it turns out that a lot of long-lasting relationships start with the woman *disliking* the guy somewhat, let alone having instant chemistry with him.

Love is not a sudden burst of energy and excitement that overwhelms your neurology in an instant. That's called a roller coaster, or a fireworks display, or infatuation. Love is the sustained, ever-deepening appreciation of another person over time. It is more like an edifice than a spectacle. It takes time to build, and once built, it tends to last a while. As Shakespeare said in *Romeo and Juliet*, "violent delights have violent ends." A fulfilling long-term relationship *may* start this way. Most don't.

Yet some women look for a cataclysmic first meeting where bells go off, firecrackers shoot around, and the earth shakes beneath her feet. He will be a prince in rust-free armor on a white horse, perfect in every way, and he will materialize to sweep her off her feet and whisk her away to the great kingdom of romance. And he'll have ballet tickets.

Perhaps this has its roots in popular Western depictions of love in movies, television, romance novels and such. What we have to realize is that these accounts of courtship are specific to Western culture. In India, where the divorce rate is lower than in America, most marriages are *arranged*. On their wedding day, the bride and groom may be meeting each other only for the first time! And yet, after time, many learn to love one another and have a lasting union.

I am not at all recommending that you go and ask your parents to find you a suitable boy and give up on the whole dating thing. What I do want is your empowerment and fulfillment. The Western romantic model of relationships is a cultural construct, and one that isn't necessarily all that successful, considering the 50% divorce rate in the United States. For something as important as fulfilling companionship, I believe you deserve better than a coin flip.

So release your attachment to the notion that you have to fall madly in love with someone in order to be fulfilled. Passion is great, romance is great, but do bring a little bit of yang into the mix – a little bit of deliberation. Madly in love is still mad, and mad people tend to make silly choices.

Now love at first sight does happen on occasion, and very rarely, you do get those butterflies in your stomach from the get-go. That's great, but just remember that there's little correlation between the butterflies and whether a man can actually be a source of lasting fulfillment for you. This is because the Prince, the perfect man, *does not exist!* Moreover, researchers show that fulfilling long-term relationships happen between partners who are more or less equal. This is called the equity theory of love. So unless you're a princess yourself, then the prince is by definition not your equal, and your partnership with him is a setup for likely failure. Eventually, a partner who feels he's bringing more to the relationship will become more demanding, impatient and dissatisfied, and the relationship founders.

Sometimes I hear from a friend that she's met 'the perfect man.' This makes me cringe a little, because often it is a prelude to heartbreak. Since the perfect man does not exist, she's expecting something that the world is not going to deliver, which is how you get pain and disappointment. Real men inhabit the real world, and the real world is a dynamic, ever-changing place. All good relationships are based on a measure of mutually acceptable compromise and influence. You mold to him a little bit, he molds to you a little bit, and we have a good fit. So even though there may not be a guy who's perfect, there is one who is perfect *for you.* And you have the power to bring that perfection about.

The perfect guy vs. the perfect guy for you

When I think of the Western idea of perfection, it's intertwined with notions of flawlessness. At its essence, it is a hard, unforgiving concept. The Eastern formulation is different and perhaps best embodied in the Zen parable of the broken cup. The Zen master says that a broken cup is perfect because it is perfect at being what it is – *a broken cup*. As long as you're not attempting to compare the broken cup to some idealized version of a cup without chips or cracks, then the broken cup is a perfect broken cup. What makes it perfect is how you look at it. If you accept the cup as it is, then it is perfect. If you expect it to be a puppy, then it is not.

All human beings are like broken cups. We are perfect at being who we are – no more, no less. And in relationships, no partner will be perfect *per se*, but some will be perfect *for you*. This softer, Eastern notion of perfection comes about when you choose to mold your mind around who a person already is. It is, in essence, a creative act, and one that requires effort.

It is also an act of forgiveness – for the perceived faults of your partner, but most importantly, forgiveness for your own faults. We tend to judge others to the same degree that we judge ourselves, so start with yourself. Realize that you and I and everyone else are all still growing in this world, and make allowance for that.

Love, in many ways, is a choice. For example, you may know someone who adopted a child, taking in a person who is a complete stranger with no blood relation and raising that individual as her own child. In workshops, I have seen how after a few minutes of exercises, two total strangers can look into each others' eyes and absolutely see one another as the beloved. So remember that you possess this gift. You don't have to pick the next guy who comes around the corner and throw yourself at him, and you don't have to be super-picky and hold out for the prince, either. You can tread the middle path – the path of the savvy woman who knows what she wants and knows where she can find it.

A big secret about how men relate to female beauty

I know women worry a fair amount about the whole beauty thing. And yes, as a guy I can assure you that looks do matter. But allow me to let you in on a little subtlety about how we view feminine beauty: *men appreciate you for what you have to offer, not what you don't.*

Let me illustrate that point. Imagine that you're hungry and someone puts a great dinner plate of broiled salmon and fresh vegetables in front of you. What's your reaction? Do you think, "Wow! This is great! Thank you so much!" Or is it, "Well, it's food, but where's the lobster and truffles? This is clearly not a dish from a 4-star restaurant!"

Most normal people would be thrilled to get the decent meal, even if it's not the best possible meal on the planet. In fact, to compare it to some dish that's not there and then have it come up short is *an act of imagination.* That requires additional effort and blood flow to the brain, which means that it effectively never happens (unless you're a big food snob). This is why almost all of us loved our college experience: we only had one, and therefore nothing to compare it to. So as far as we know, it was the best college experience possible!

A man will appreciate you for what you have to offer, not what you don't.

So when you're with a guy who's into you, and it's just you and him – which is most of the time you're together – he's not going to sweat the little physical things *you* think matter. He's too busy celebrating your company! He doesn't care about your butt size, thigh size, breast size, less-than-flawless hair or any of that. That stuff comes up, if ever, only when he's comparing you to other women -- and there are no women around! And if you are the one who makes him feel like a million bucks, then even when there are other women around, he secretly knows that you're his gem that no one else has. And if he's in love with you, you automatically become the most beautiful woman in the world.

Now let's examine the converse scenario. Let's assume you're a contestant in the Miss Universe contest. Ever seen one of those shows? Now, even though a guy would be thrilled to be with any one of those young, beautiful women, when there's a bevy of 100 of them, he's going to start to get picky. And suddenly Miss Venezuela doesn't look so great because she was standing next to Miss Brazil, who's more his type.

When you go out with a group of very attractive girlfriends, or head out to a place like a nightclub where everybody's all gussied up, you're putting yourself in a pageant-like situation. This puts you at an instant disadvantage, since it makes it much more likely that you'll be standing next to Miss Brazil, who may very well be more his type.

So emphasize your strengths and leave alone the rest. Do your best to interact one-on-one with a man who interests you. And for crying out loud, don't invite comparison or ask him what his type is. If he's with you, you're his type. And he appreciates you for what you are, not what you aren't.

He doesn't care that much about your shoes or dress
Here's another little secret: as long as you're presentable and alluring, men don't really pay all that much attention to the specifics of what you're wearing. A man will be happy as long as your outfit is elegant and flattering.

So if you want to keep up with fashion or impress your girlfriends, go ahead, as long as you keep in mind that what's fashionable isn't necessarily what men find appealing. So if you want to dress for your girlfriends, be fashionable. If you want to attract men, wear something elegant that emphasizes your best features, regardless of what's in fashion at the time.

Your secret gift as a woman

The good news is that, as a woman, you are designed to see beyond short-term attractiveness (or unattractiveness) of a man to recognize what is deeper and more meaningful. For better or for worse, men are designed to put a lot of importance upon a woman's appearance. Things like hip-to-waist ratio, complexion and youthful appearance are surface proxies that evolution has chosen to signal fertility – and thus, desirability – in a woman. Anecdotally, it is rare to see a handsome, well-to-do man with a woman who is not outwardly attractive, which bears out this point in the real world.

The converse situation, on the other hand, is common: very attractive women routinely associate and marry men who are not nearly as physically attractive. Scientists believe that this is because during the course of human evolution, the survival of human offspring depended very much on the cooperation of the male partner. Human infants are remarkably helpless, requiring nurturance for the better part of two decades before they can thrive on their own. As such, the women who were very good at choosing male partners who were strong, reliable, long-term providers had offspring that did disproportionately better than the women who did not have that skill. Those genes got passed on, and here we are.

This is a crude sketch of why women are willing to overlook certain characteristics in men, and we have seen enough versions of the rich older man/attractive younger woman couple to know that it is borne out in reality. What you have to remember is that this is your gift as a woman. It is part of the design of the universe, part of the Tao, that for you, beauty is more a feeling than a sight. If a man makes you feel good, he will look good in your eyes. Feeling good is the essence of fulfillment, so you have the extraordinary luck to be able to find fulfillment in all kinds of unexpected places.

> **As a woman, you possess the extraordinary gift of making a man who makes you feel good look good.**

The more you use the Tao, the more you move with the Tao, the more it brings fulfillment to your life. So be patient with yourself and with the men you meet. If you actually enjoyed the company of a man, allow that to take its course. See what happens for another meeting or two, even if thunderbolts did not descend from the heavens during the first date and he did not have a halo around his head by the end of it. Love visits at unlikely moments. And as Williamson said memorably in *A Return to Love*, there is one mistake in life, and that is not to let love in. At the same time, chemistry (or more accurately, a certain chemical compatibility) is an essential part of any relationship and you will ignore it only to your peril. As we will discuss later, listen to what your body is telling you.

Types of men

There are as many types of men as there are males on this planet, so it's unwise to pigeonhole a man and close his case. At the same time, there are some useful classifications for figuring out who you're dealing with. The purpose of the following archetypes is to increase your awareness and help you answer the following question: "How likely is this man to be a source of long-term fulfillment for me?"

I like the heart and spine classification because of its simplicity. It gets down to what really matters in a man. Here are the four categories and some types that you may encounter in each:

No heart, no spine. Needless to say, this is not the kind of person you'd want to involve yourself with. If you were meant to hang out with jellyfish, you'd live in the ocean.

Lots of heart, not a lot of spine. This is the nice guy. He can communicate his feelings, he's in touch with his feminine side, and in the end, he will annoy you because he either doesn't stand up for himself or have clear direction and purpose in life. Earlier, we called him Lance.

Lots of spine, not a lot of heart. Stands up for himself just fine – and mostly just for himself. Bad boys fall in this category, as do macho men, successful and super-driven businessmen who have no time for you, and all manner of bullies and petty tyrants. We called him Biff in Chapter 4.

Plenty of spine, plenty of heart. This is the domain of the Good Guy, or Victor as we dubbed him.

Why good women get involved (and stay) in bad relationships

When I was younger, I always noticed that many of my beautiful, accomplished, sweet and brilliant female friends dated men who did not treat them nearly well enough. Turns out that powerful reasons drive such phenomena, so my friends weren't entirely crazy. Once you know why good women end up dating jerks, then you can use your awareness to prevent such a thing from happening in the future to yourself or a friend.

Some of why good women end up in bad relationships has to do with their self-concepts and self-esteem. And some of why they stay in them has to do with what I call the *slot machine model* of human behavior and *sunk costs*. Let's talk about the slot machines first.

The slot machine model of human behavior

Let's say you're in Las Vegas, and you've decided to play a slot machine. You put in a coin, pull the lever, and – nothing. Well, that's fine – you weren't expecting to win immediately anyway. So you put in another coin and – nothing again. In fact, nothing is the most likely outcome every time. Funny that.

But before you know it, you've sunk quite a few coins in this machine. Now you're thinking, "I'm invested; I can't just quit now! I've fattened this thing up – it's going to pay off any second now! Jackpot city!"

The fact remains that the most likely outcome of your next pull (and the next, and the next, and the next) is still nothing. And that likelihood does not change whether you put in one coin or 10,000 coins before this pull.

Psychologists have noticed that one of the reasons why this happens (and why casinos are making a mint) is that the human mind grasps poorly the concept of *sunk costs*.

Those first 100 coins that you put into the machine are gone forever, and they have no bearing upon the outcome of the next pull of the lever. People tend to mistake the sunk cost for an *investment*, which has an expectation of future payoff commensurate with the investment. A sunk cost, on the other hand, is just plain gone.

The way this concept plays out in a bad relationship is that the aggrieved party thinks that she has *invested* two years dating a jerk, so she can't just throw that investment away. Besides, through her efforts, he might reform and thereby reward her with the jackpot she's been working on all along.

Well, there is no way to retrieve or throw away those two years – they're gone for good. They are *sunk costs*. And the jackpot isn't coming. Just as in playing a slot machine, the best policy once you realize you're in a sunk cost situation is to cut and run and immediately stop your losses. The sooner a woman leaves behind the jerk, the sooner she's opening her life to the arrival of a guy (perhaps even a Good Guy) who can be a catalyst of fulfillment.

Why does this happen? I can think of a few reasons. The first has to do with a hormone called *oxytocin*. As far as we can tell so far, oxytocin has three main functions: it promotes powerful contractions of the uterus to expel the infant during childbirth; it promotes breastfeeding; and it creates a sense of bonding. The bigger the dose of oxytocin, the greater the sense of bonding. The whopping dose of oxytocin that bathes the brain during childbirth is part of the reason why mothers remain deeply in love with their babies for life.

An interesting feature of oxytocin is that it is released as a result of touch and at the moment of orgasm. So whenever a woman gets sexually intimate with a man, especially when she experiences an orgasm with him, she is bonding with him more closely. This bonding occurs at a deep, unconscious level and no amount of rational thought can undo it. In fact, psychologists conducted a study showing that a small whiff of oxytocin administered nasally was enough to make people far more trusting of total strangers (Kosfeld et al., 2005).

So if you're one of those good women who has been spending far too much time with a bad match, consider whether it is your good sense speaking or the oxytocin. Like any hormone or drug, withdrawal results in exponential decay of the effects. So one way of breaking the bond between you and Mr. Wrong is to stay away from him. A trip is often an excellent idea.

The reason why good women end up with bad men in the first place (and stay with them) has much to do with self-esteem and the self-concept.

The self-concept and how it affects your relationships

How you perceive yourself has a significant effect on the companions you pick and the relationships you have. *Self-concepts* are the beliefs and judgments we have about ourselves. Some of them are objective: "I am a 32-year old female." Some are subjective: "I am likable." *Self-esteem* is one of those subjective aspects of the self-concept, corresponding roughly to how much we like ourselves.

Psychological research shows that in the context of relationships, our self-concepts try to fulfill two functions. First is to seek feedback from others that *enhances* the self-concept. Second is to seek feedback that is *consistent* with the self-concept (Sedikides & Strube, 1997).

It's easy to understand why we would seek out compliments and positive feedback that make us feel good about ourselves and allow us to see ourselves as attractive and competent. But what about consistency? Turns out that we all have a strong drive to avoid cognitive dissonance by seeking out a world that is consistent with our beliefs. As stated by psychologist Carol Brehm, "our self-concepts... make life predictable and sustain coherent expectations about what each day will bring." Without them, "social life would be a confusing, chaotic jumble."

Now here's where things get interesting. If you happen to *like* yourself, then the self-enhancement drive coincides with the self-consistency drive, and all is well. If you're around people who are saying nice things about you, then you are getting the self-enhancement ("You're great!") that is consistent with your self-concept, which is that you're a nice person ("I'm great!"). Life is hunky-dory.

However, if you *don't* happen to like yourself very well, you run into a problem. Psychologists find that you will still like getting praise and compliments from others – this much seems to be an automatic, unconscious response. But once you have a chance to think about it, you will come to distrust the positive feedback (Swann et al., 1990).

How does this affect your romantic life? It seems that in the context of *dating*, self-enhancement is the primary drive, and everyone likes companions who are supportive, kind and accepting of who we are. However, for long-term, *committed* relationships, self-consistency becomes more important. This is such a prevalent phenomenon that it even has a name: the *marriage shift* (Swann et al., 1994).

The way this plays out is rather interesting (and may even sound familiar). If a person has good self-esteem, then hallelujah – she will gravitate towards people who accept and cherish her as she is and tend to stay with those people.

However, if she has a negative self-concept, initially, she will enjoy the compliments and positive feedback. But over time, the self-consistency instinct will rise up and ask questions along the lines of, "Well, he can't *really* believe I'm that great. What's wrong with *him*?"

Eventually, the dissonance between the positive feedback she's receiving and the low self-concept will be so great that it creates feelings of inauthenticity and distrust ("He's just saying this stuff; he can't possibly be sincere") and leads to the dissolution of the relationship.

This is part of the reason why those wonderful female friends of mine dated and even married men who treated them poorly. Those women were not crazy; they were simply ending up with men who fulfilled their self-concept.

If you can look back on your long-term relationships and count off a series of partners whose treatment of you made all your friends scratch their heads, then the problem may lie with your self-esteem.

How to improve your self-esteem

The good news is that self-concepts can change, and you can enhance your self-esteem even if you think it's a little low (but not rock-bottom). The ease with which someone can change her self-concept has to do with how sure she is with her self-concept right now (Swann & Ely, 1984). If she's convinced she's totally unworthy, that's tough to turn around. Luckily, that's rare, and even people who have low self-esteem only *suspect* that they're total dweebs but aren't quite sure. In that case, here are two things that can turn your self-esteem around.

Allow positive feedback. Even if you start out with low self-esteem, kind words from an adoring lover can turn that around in short order as you start to enjoy and even believe what he says. So whenever you hear a compliment, stop, take it in, and allow it to sink in. Resist the reflex downer comments like, "Well, you don't really mean that" or "Well sure I have nice hair but look what a mess it is." Just *take* the darned compliment and say only "Thank you." Or even better, "You're absolutely right – thank you." Positive feedback from others also helps, so surround yourself with appreciative people who prop you up and spend less time with those who bring you down. The compliments are coming at you all the time if you only pay attention, so -- pay attention! And accept them with open arms.

Engage in service. We get a lot of our sense of self-esteem by how useful we feel we are. So go ahead and make yourself useful! Nobody's stopping you. Tutor some kids, volunteer at a shelter, sign up as a Big Sister, help out at church. Go to a website like volunteermatch.org and find a project you can pour yourself into.

There is no faster way to feel worthy than to serve. Not only will you feel like your services are useful and necessary, you will also exercise dormant talents which you may have never thought you had. And scientists have shown that altruistic behavior actually lights up your brain's pleasure center. In his book *Why Good Things Happen to Good People*, Professor of Bioethics Stephen Post has shown that people who volunteer benefit from improved mood, reduced anxiety and depression, better relationships, and even increased lifespan. Doing good makes you feel good every time. And it's a lot cheaper (and safer) than drugs.

How to spot bad boys

We talked about noticing aspects of your own behavior that are relevant to your fulfillment. For example, if you're chronically getting in the way of your own happiness through self-deprecation, that's useful to know (and, by the way, stop doing that already. Thanks.). Equally important is to notice behaviors of potential male companions which bear on your fulfillment.

This section is for those of you who find yourselves occasionally (or serially) involved with bad boys only to regret the episode afterwards. If you've never had a problem with bad boys and don't think you ever will, you may also skip this section. If you like bad boys and can handle them just fine, then skip this section. If you've ever found a bad boy even slightly appealing and think you *could* someday get involved with one, read on.

There's something attractive about bad boys, which is why smart women need to be able to spot them *before* getting involved with one, because they're just so darn tasty sometimes. In a way, getting involved with a bad boy is like obesity: prevention is the best solution. If it's already happened, it's often too late, and the solutions are laborious and ineffective. So unless you're signing up for a relationship of limited duration with a definite expiration date, you're better off avoiding the bad boy.

Also, because of the particularly heady brew of chemicals bad boys induce in your head and body, getting involved with a bad boy makes it more difficult to recognize and appreciate a Good Guy. Don't tell me I didn't warn you.

My definition of a bad boy is simple: he is a boy (as opposed to a man) who is bad for you in the long term. By *bad* I mean that overall, he will bring more pain to your life than joy. Don't get me wrong: there will be some good times with the bad boy. That's why women get involved with them. But the *net result* tends to be more pain than joy.

By *you* I mean the whole of your life: your mental, spiritual, physical and financial well-being. No one item here absolutely certifies a person as a bad boy; however, the occurrence of several of these characteristics in one individual should be a warning sign.

Incidentally, a man's number of sexual partners is not necessarily an indicator of whether he's a bad boy or not.

This is all about how he treats *you* in the long term. It would be just as foolish to let go of a sexually experienced man who loves you and treats you like the queen of the universe as it would be to attach yourself to a monk who disrespects you. In any case, always expect a genuinely desirable man to have been noticed by women before you.

If I were to pick one quality that would be the most accurate indicator of whether someone's a bad boy, it's a presence of *extremes*. Whether of beauty, wealth, intelligence, tidiness, messiness, neglect or solicitude, extremes are tipoffs that this guy might be a handful who'll bring you more trouble than it's worth. The Tao is about taking the middle path; those who court extremes are not with the Tao. If you bring those people into your life, you may be inviting instability and trouble. Chapter 13 of the *Tao Te Ching* says:

> *What does it mean that success is as dangerous as failure?*
> *Whether you go up the ladder or down it,*
> *You position is shaky.*
> *When you stand with your two feet on the ground,*
> *You will always keep your balance.*

Every characteristic listed here is like a double-edged sword: the very thing that makes it appealing can also render it detrimental. The list is intended to make you aware and wary of whether you're signing up for the fun or the pain. Whenever you spot one of these list items, ask yourself: "What's the purpose of this behavior? What's he trying to get out of it?" Put yourself in his motorcycle boots for a moment, and you'll gain instant insight into the male mind.

Don't get me wrong -- bad boys can be a lot of fun, and the totally nice guys might be pretty deathly boring. The purpose of this is, first and foremost, your awareness so you can choose a middle path. You want a guy who has a little bit of an edge and is decent to boot.

Here are some behaviors that could mean you're dealing with a bad boy, and how your mind may rationalize it as appealing rather than problematic. *Caveat emptor.*

Moving things along too quickly. Bad boys tend to make early declarations of affection – genuinely or for effect. They also fall in love easily and have no problem proposing a romantic weekend getaway when they've known you for less than fifteen minutes.

What it looks like: Spontaneity and joie de vivre.

What it could really be: Impulsiveness; trying to get into your pants as swiftly as possible

What you're signing up for if you date him: plans only made at the last minute; plans cancelled at the last minute; general irresponsibility; similarly impulsive overtures to other women.

Being just a tad too smooth. When you first meet him, does he touch you too early and too often? Is he whispering in your ear? Is he overly generous with his compliments? Does he attempt to take you away from your friends and get you alone? Is he always subtly (or blatantly) pushing the boundary of what's appropriate and comfortable? Is he telling stories that seem too well-rehearsed and designed to aggrandize him, impress you, and get you worked up? Is there a lot of showmanship going on? Once you've started dating, are his excuses for marginal behavior all too plausible? If so, you are almost certainly dealing with a bad boy.

What it looks like: Romance! These men know that this is the ultimate bait for getting a woman, and therefore use it skillfully and without apology.

What it could really be: Too good to be true is almost always exactly that. Deliberately seductive behavior usually means you're dealing with an experienced player.

What you're signing up for if you date him: sexual infidelity (and possibly diseases); unreliability; rapid emotional detachment once he's gotten what he wants from you.

Thrillseeking behavior. He rides a motorcycle – a big Harley, actually. He skydives, takes all kinds of drugs, drinks a lot, goes out five times a week or more, and generally looks for the adrenaline rush.

What it looks like: A life of excitement that you want to be a part of.

What it could really be: Although many grown, responsible men take calculated risks, chronic thrillseeking is often a sign of immaturity and recklessness.

What you're signing up for if you date him: worry; genuine fear; loneliness as he goes off on his jaunts; infidelity; irresponsibility; run-ins with the law.

Devil-may-care attitude. He lives by his own rules – and *only* by his own rules. He dresses like he wants, works when he wants, eats what he wants, says what he wants. 'No one will the boss of me' is his motto.

What it looks like: Fierce, roguish independence.

What it could really be: Lack of consideration and antisocial behavior, which will inevitably extend to you as well.

What you're signing up for if you date him: inability to make plans, or broken plans when he does make them; verbal abuse; insensitivity to your feelings and desires; financial distress.

Studied physical appearance. A stylish man is good to find. However, you can tell if a man has spent more time than normal on his appearance for effect. Too disheveled

goes in the same category as too slick: extremes are what you're watching out for. Heavy cologne is often a tip-off.
What it looks like: Style, baby, style.
What it could really be: Narcissism and vanity.
What you're signing up for if you date him: Player tendencies; mistreatment; self-absorption.

General evasiveness. When a man is evasive about personal questions – especially about dating, the women in his life, the length of relationships and such – beware. He *may* be doing it for sport, but chances are he has something to hide. A good relationship is based on honesty, trust and respect. Chronic evasiveness precludes all three, so this is an inauspicious start to things. Incidentally, if a man lies to you even once for non-humanitarian reasons (e.g., only something like "There's no one hiding in the attic from the secret police" is acceptable), that's grounds for leaving him.
What it looks like: Mystery and intrigue.
What it could really be: Skeletons in the closet.
What you're signing up for if you date him: Unreliability; mistrust; lies.

Living space that's too well thought-out or too messy. Psychologists talk about the concept of *thin-slicing*: how from one snapshot of a person's life you can intuit fairly accurate information about his character. In fact, psychologists showed in an experiment that walking through a person's uninhabited apartment yielded a more accurate character assessment than an interview with that person (Gosling et al., 2002).

As such, the well-appointed love nest and the messy bachelor pad are both potential signs of trouble ahead. A man's chic apartment with the bearskin rug in front of the fireplace, four-poster canopied bed, strategically positioned

Art of Sensual Massage on the coffee table and scented candles everywhere should make you wonder why he created this ambience from which a woman would supposedly find it difficult to escape – and how many women preceded you and will succeed you. On the other end of the spectrum, the dishevelment of the messy apartment should make you wonder whether that's the level of consideration with which he'll be treating you.

What it looks like: Good taste (love nest), endearingly boyish disorder (messy bachelor pad).

What it could really be: A player.

What you're signing up for if you date him: See 'Being too smooth' entry above.

Lack of consideration. Did he ask you out far enough in advance so you'd be able to make plans? Did he call ahead of time to say he was going to be late? Did he open your car door for you? Did he offer to pay when he invited you out? Did he ask about your sick cat when you said she was sick? How about your sick grandmother? How about when *you* were sick? Does he offer you his coat when you look cold? I'm belaboring the point here, and what I'm saying is this: you know what consideration looks like, and it's different from when a guy's being a jerk to you. Any *one* of these things is not a big deal, but a bunch of them happening in close succession is a sign of trouble.

What it looks like: Non-conformity, roguish independence.

What it could really be: A jerk.

What you're signing up for if you date him: see *Devil-may-care attitude* above.

Indecision. This is one of the characteristics that truly separates the men from the boys: can he decide? Decision means leadership, leadership means responsibility, and responsibility means *power*. An indecisive man is a powerless man. If he waffles and weaves with every decision he makes, or even worse, consults you for all his decisions, *run*. Better a man who decides and is wrong on occasion than one who refuses to decide at all. Of all the characteristics mentioned here, this may very well be the worst. Just stay away.

What it looks like: Sensitivity and consideration.

What it could really be: Spinelessness, weakness.

What you're signing up if you date him: Exasperation, ruined plans, total disaster.

Highly selective availability or too much availability. Again, you have to ask yourself why this is the case, because there are usually good reasons for extreme unavailability or availability. A man with highly selective availability is often seeing other women or married to one. A man who's always available may be unemployed or desperate. Either way, keep your eyes open.

What it looks like: Busy, important man-about-town (unavailable one) or a guy who's really, really into you (highly available one).

What it could really be: A man with too many options or too few.

What you're signing up for if you date him: A man who will either keep you hanging on or will be always hanging on you.

How to spot Good Guys

We've discussed how to spot the kind of man you'd rather avoid. How about the kind of man you would *want* to have in your life – the Good Guy? Here's a field guide to spotting the keepers. What's interesting about these characteristics is that they are harder to spot than the ones for the Bad Boys. It will take more time and effort to discover the Good Guy's best qualities precisely because of the kind of person he is. Treasures are often buried. The bigger they are, the more digging they require.

It's unlikely that any one person will have all of these characteristics at once. Moreover, to get *too* picky about the kind of man you want to associate with would be a negation of the principle of abundance. The purpose of this list is to prime your conscious and subconscious mind such that when one of these features pops up, you will know what it means.

Sense of purpose. This is the foundational characteristic of the mature masculine and the source of the Good Guy's power. Since the Good Guy is the embodiment of the mature masculine, then he will always have a strong sense of purpose and direction in his life. He knows what he's doing with his life and why and has a plan for achieving his goals.
Signs to look for: Has set and achieved a number of life goals; has a list of goals, written or not, that he'd like to achieve; fills his time with activities that are aligned with his purpose.

Humility. Although he is aware of his own powers, he is also aware that the world is much bigger than he is. This grounds him, giving him a great sense of awe and humility. He recognizes that his talents are a tool for service to the world, as opposed to an instrument for self-aggrandizement and appeasing his ego.
Signs to look for: Mild tendency towards self-effacement; underreporting his achievements; greater interest in talking about you rather than himself.

Decisiveness. A Good Guy knows that his job is to take care of things. Since part of that involves making lots of decisions, he has gotten good at that. He trusts his instincts and renders decisions efficiently. He would rather make a decision quickly and then change his mind rather than dwell on it until it's too late. Because of his decisiveness and the quality of his decision-making, people around him come to trust him, too. In the presence of a trustworthy man, the divine feminine has a chance to relax and express itself.

Signs to look for: Makes decisions efficiently without dithering.

Trustworthiness. A Good Guy's word is a Good Guy's honor. If he says he's going to call you in two days, he calls you in two days. If he says he's going to pick you up at 7:15, he shows up at 7:15.

Signs to look for: Does what he says when he says he's going to do it; gets genuinely angry on occasion without trying to sugarcoat it or suppress the anger.

Consideration. Lao Tzu says in Chapter 67 of the *Tao Te Ching*:

> *I have just three things to teach:*
> *simplicity, patience, compassion.*

The way people manifest compassion is in their ability to put themselves in someone else's shoes. The way people show that in their behavior is in what we call *consideration*. We hold the door open for someone walking in behind us because we know a door in our face is no fun and do not want someone else to experience that. Similarly, a compassionate man will demonstrate consideration towards you and everyone else around him, from the waiter to the parking valet to an employee.

Signs to look for: Does all the things thought of as well-mannered; remembers birthdays, anniversaries, and your preferences and does something about them; tips well; treats subordinates well; gets along with kids.

Strong internal compass. The chief feature that distinguishes a man from a boy is the same as what distinguishes a woman from a girl: an internal frame of reference. When a man has a strong internal frame of reference, he makes decisions based on what constitutes *his* fulfillment, as opposed to looking to outside sources for approval. For better or for worse, one of these outside sources is sometimes *you.* Therefore, somewhat paradoxically, the Good Guy is not the one who caters to your every whim and desire, but rather the one who has his own enlightened self-interest in mind.

Part of being the embodiment of the divine masculine involves the ability to stand firm amidst the passions and vicissitudes of the divine feminine, the most likely source of which will be you. The man who easily bends to your will, then, is not necessarily the one you want (you *will* get bored with him – trust me on this one). The one who listens to you, weathers the storm of your passion, and still renders rational decisions based on what's best for everyone in the long term, is a much better bet. You may not necessarily agree with him all the time, but you do respect him for his solidity. This breeds further trust and allows the flourishing of the divine feminine in you.

Signs to look for: Stands up for himself without being argumentative; is not afraid to contradict you (in a non-hysterical way) on occasion.

Equanimity. The Good Guy is a calm man. He keeps his cool even when the world presents challenges to him – *especially* when the world presents challenges to him. Things just don't *bother* him that much. The way he handles challenges is not through whining or complaining, but rather through action (see *decisiveness* entry above). Very rarely he

105

may get angry about something that genuinely upsets him, but he does not dwell on it. Although he is a passionate individual, he has learned how to channel his passion in an organized, constructive way.

Signs to look for: Grace in the presence or absence of pressure.

As a side note, you're probably noticing how all these characteristics dovetail into one another. Equanimity is related to the internal compass, which in turn relates to decisiveness. Humility and compassion go hand-in-hand and are related to the last feature: acceptance.

Acceptance. One of the central principles of Taoist philosophy is accepting the world as it is instead of trying to struggle against it. Chapter 29 of the *Tao Te Ching*, one of my favorite which I have drawn upon several times in this book, expresses this principle succinctly:

> *Do you want to improve the world?*
> *I don't think it can be done.*
>
> *The world is sacred.*
> *It can't be improved.*
> *If you tamper with it, you'll ruin it.*
> *If you treat it like an object, you'll lose it.*
>
> *There is a time for being ahead,*
> *A time for being behind;*
> *A time for being in motion,*
> *A time for being at rest;*
> *A time for being vigorous,*
> *A time for being exhausted;*
> *A time for being safe,*
> *A time for being in danger.*

The Master sees things as they are,
Without trying to control them.
She lets them go their own way,
And resides at the center of the circle.

The Good Guy understands this. Therefore he accepts himself. From Chapter 30 of the *Tao Te Ching*:

The Master does his job
And then stops.
He understands that the universe
Is forever out of control,
And that trying to dominate events
Goes against the current of the Tao.
Because he believes in himself,
He doesn't try to convince others.
Because he is content with himself,
He doesn't need others' approval.
Because he accepts himself,
The whole world accepts him.

Because he accepts himself fully, he is able to accept you fully. This means that he will not try to fix you – he will have chosen you because you are already what he desires. He will not rail against the world because it does not conform to his will. Rather, he will flow with it.
Signs to look for: being comfortable in his own skin and generally tolerant of others.

The Good Guy's secret turn-on

I'm about to let you in on a big secret on how to make the dating dance significantly easier and more fun for yourself, especially if you find it a challenge to meet men.

And the secret is this: an available man loves to be approached by a woman. Especially if he is the right kind of man.

What women do not realize is that men are terrified of rejection. I have spoken and written to thousands of them, and that is by far their biggest fear in dating. So even though they may look like invincible hulks of self-confidence on the outside, all of them secretly cower inside at your power to utter that dread syllable: "NO."

This explains why you have so many men who have taken considerable time and effort to show up to a venue and then spend the next three hours chatting with their male buddies or twisting swizzle sticks instead of meeting the nice ladies who are there specifically to meet them.

Recently, I asked ten thousand of my male readers to recount a specific episode where a woman did something that was particularly appealing. The answers all boiled down to two things: *showing appreciation* and *taking initiative*. So taking the initiative turns out to be one of the most attractive things you can do when interacting with a man. In Chapter 9, we will elaborate on how to make it incredibly easy to get the interaction started with any man practically anywhere.

Good Guys love it when you take initiative.

The dilemma of dating the Great Man

Some of you will have the opportunity to date truly extraordinary men. These are men who have excelled in their fields of endeavor, be it science, art, spirituality, leadership, business, or sports, and may have even achieved some renown. They aren't just Good Guys – they're *really* Good Guys. Let's call them Great Men.

Should you have the opportunity to get involved with one of these Great Men, there's something you need to know. The extreme manifestation of any trait tends to become its own opposite. And so when a Good Guy becomes really, *really* good, he becomes in effect – you guessed it – a bad boy.

Let me illustrate. If he's a powerful guy and very sociable, he's going to be very smooth. Because he doesn't have a lot of time and he's used to getting his way, he'll want to move things along quickly. Because he likes to challenge himself, he's likely to be a thrillseeker. He's a powerful guy, so he's not going to care too much what others think of him. He's a man of status, power and perhaps wealth that other women have noticed, so he's going to have some options for companionship. So for all the world he looks like a bad boy on the surface.

Greatness is both boon and burden, and it will always impinge upon the close relationships of the Great Man. The rewards of being with a Great Man can be significant, so if you have the patience and strength to put up with the burdens, perhaps it's right for you. I'm not here to prescribe you a course of action, but rather to increase your awareness so you can make better decisions.

Every Great Man may not be a pain in the rear, but it happens often enough to be worth mentioning. My job is to ensure that you are as well-informed as possible, and so I want you to know what you're signing up for when you choose to get involved with a Great Man – specifically, a bit of trouble. Gandhi beat his wife, neglected his family and got himself assassinated, which is enough to ruin any relationship. Martin Luther King and John F. Kennedy philandered and made their share of enemies. Any number of renowned composers, musicians, artists and writers seriously tried their partners' patience with various excesses. It's up to you to pick the kind of trouble you're willing to put up with and to find it exhilarating or annoying. Every relationship involves a degree of compromise; just know what you're getting yourself into.

Part II
Be

Chapter 6. Beliefs

How to keep a healthy mental diet

We all know that for optimum health, it's important to eat well and avoid junk food. It's called junk food for a reason: it tends to be high in fat and sugar and low in the nutrients that your body truly needs to flourish and thrive. The same principle applies to your mental health. To maintain a robust mind that continues to serve your growth and development, you must feed it the right kind of food.

Edible food comes through your mouth, and mental food comes through your eyes and ears. Books, magazines, radio, movies, television, billboards and the like are the substance of this food. While we have a fair amount of control over what food we ingest, controlling what enters through our eyes and ears tends to be trickier. "The eye it cannot choose but see,/ We cannot bid the ear be still," as William Wordsworth once said.

We should not underestimate the potency of mental food. If you are reading this now, this means that you learned the fundamentals of a language – man's most complex invention – simply by catching the syllables wafting in the air from your parents to you. If you have a skill at work or play a musical instrument, this is because you received the proper mental food at some point in your life. Your brain then turned this food into learning, which it later used to turn into action. The mental food you have ingested has largely determined who you are today.

In college and medical school, I was training as a scientist and, as such, tended to dismiss talk about the power of the unconscious mind, subliminal messages and other such pseudoscientific-sounding things. I had a robust belief in the power of my conscious mind to filter things out and selectively let in only what I *chose* to let in. As such, things like violent movies and pessimistic people were not going to affect me, because I wouldn't let them. Or so I thought.

As I delved deeper in the scientific literature, I found that the influence of the information we allow casually to enter our psyche is real and substantial. Many psychological experiments demonstrate this very elegantly.

Psychologist John Bargh did an experiment in which subjects were asked to make sentences out of a list of jumbled words as quickly as possible, ostensibly being tested for speed and accuracy. In fact, there were two tests: one which contained words such as 'grey', 'bingo', 'wrinkle', 'old', and 'Florida', and another which contained no such words. What the experimenters were really measuring was not performance on the quiz, but the time it took for the subjects to leave the testing room and to get to the front door of the building after completing the quiz.

What they found was both startling and enlightening: those who had words in their quizzes connoting old age got to the front door about 30% slower than those who didn't. This means that for a brief interval following the quiz sprinkled with those words, *they behaved as if they had gotten older.*

Eating disorders owe much of their prevalence to mass media, especially television. Dr Anne Becker, director of the Harvard Eating Disorders Center, studied adolescent women in a remote area of Fiji. She found that just three years after the introduction of television, 69% of the girls were on a diet or had some kind of eating disorder. Prior to that, no one even *knew* what a diet was. 83% said that television influenced the way they felt about their bodies.

If that result does not surprise you, consider this study conducted by psychologist Ellen Langer of Harvard. She gathered a group of elderly patients. She put them in a nursing-home like environment, but with a twist: she gave them clothing to wear from when they were in their twenties. She also piped in radio programs, played TV shows from that time and left around copies of *Life* magazine all from that time and even stocked the refrigerator with long-discontinued foods with labels from that era.

Guess what happened to the patients? When Dr Langer did physical exams on them after the experiment, they had tighter skin, better eyesight, less joint pain, increased muscle strength and even higher bone density than before compared to the control group.

This is no joke here: things as fundamental as *bone density and eyesight* actually improved – just by being in an environment that constantly reminded them to be younger. So deliberately create the environment for yourself that's conducive to your growth and well-being, and eliminate the mental food that undercuts it.

The good news is that we do exert a fair amount of control over the mental food we allow into our psyche. You can control whether or not you watch TV, listen to the radio, go to a movie, pick up a book or read a magazine. Once you choose to expose yourself to these media, you can pick what kind you listen to, read or watch.

Long-term fulfillment and happiness have their roots in a calm mind. Inner peace is a habit that needs to be cultivated – no one is born with it. There are enough forces in the world attempting to jostle your mind; they do not need your help in creating further turmoil.

Cultivate a peaceful mindset

If you are reading this book now, chances are you have an abiding interest in achieving a lasting, deep inner peace. If so, you may wish to consider taking a look at your mental diet. Most media is supported by advertising. Advertising is designed to make you buy stuff, and it accomplishes this by making you feel inadequate. The message, implicit or explicit, is that without the object of desire in the advertisement, your life is incomplete: you *need* this.

The truth is different: *you have everything that you need.* Everything. If you're reading this right now, you are probably clothed and well-fed, with a roof over your head, caring family and friends, and enough free time and resources to be reading in the first place. You also have a working heart, kidneys, intestines, muscles, bone and a magnificent brain – literally trillions of cells working in concert to make every second of your existence possible, even when you are sound asleep. Sure, you may not have a custom designer wardrobe, a personal cook, or a villa in Tuscany, but those are not things that you *need*. You have everything that you need, and miraculously so.

Going back to the beliefs that we discussed, if the world is truly a reflection of you and your dominant thoughts, then knowing beyond a shadow of a doubt that you have everything that you need puts you in a mindset of self-sufficiency and abundance. This in turn makes the world respond to you with abundance. The converse of this would be to approach the world with the attitude "If only I had..." or "I don't have enough of...", which is the sure formula for the world saying right back to you, "You're absolutely right – your life is inadequate," thereby inviting more of that imagined inadequacy into your life. You get more of what you focus on.

It may be a good idea to excise the following items from your mental diet permanently. Some of these suggestions may seem a little radical. However, *extraordinary results require extraordinary measures.* Even a single issue of a magazine can hammer an insidious message into your unconscious mind hundreds of times, making the message virtually irresistible.

Moreover, I *promise* you will not miss these items once you get rid of them. In fact, we hardly ever miss things that aren't there at all – we only miss things that have an intermittent presence in your life. It's good to think of them as training wheels or crutches – once you can function without them, you're actually far better off without them, since they tend to get in the way. Here are some crutches you can get rid of:

Magazines, especially women's fashion magazines. Fashion magazines are particularly insidious because under the guise of helping you out, they actually do a lot more damage than good. There are many reasons for this.

First, the women portrayed in these magazines are usually models, who have a body composition very different from the average woman. Average height for a female model is 5'8" (172cm), and weight 105-120 lbs (47-54 kg). If you happen to have that body type, you are lucky enough to live in an era where the fashion for female beauty happens to coincide with your particular form. Otherwise, less than 5% of women are that tall, and for their height, models are on average 23% underweight. In fact, the average North American woman is 5'4" tall (163cm) and weighs 140 lbs (63.5kg).

Although the pictures don't state explicitly that "this is what you're supposed to look like", looking at hundreds of pictures of women with these unusual physiques will leave an unmistakable impression on your mind. For the sake of experiment, I just went through the fall fashion issue of a prominent women's fashion magazine. In its 506 pages, I counted 478 pictures of female models. How would you feel if someone hinted at you 478 times that you don't look good?

Moreover, if you have met a model in person, you may have noticed another curious fact: they look different from their digitally-altered photos. As such, the ideal perpetuated by these publications is often not only unattainable, but *nonexistent!* Even models themselves don't look like models. As someone who has lived in Los Angeles for many years and has met many such models in person, I can attest to the truth of that statement. As Naomi Wolf once stated eloquently, "We as women are *trained* to see ourselves as cheap imitations of fashion photographs, rather than seeing fashion photographs as cheap imitations of women." Time to de-train your brain.

Second, the advertisements in these publications often promote fashion items. Like the weather, fashion changes by definition, and you are expected to keep up with it by buying the items depicted in the ads. The implication is that your adequacy depends upon your purchase of these items. Yet the target moves constantly, the items becoming obsolete soon after you buy them. In fact, that's how the fashion industry thrives – making perfectly functional stuff obsolete so you have to buy new stuff. Elegance and style are great ideas; however, they are different from being *fashionable*, and you could easily spend all your time and energy chasing down that elusive ideal, which, like the horizon, you will never catch. To paraphrase Williamson, *you* support the fashion industry, but it does not tend to support you back.

Moreover, some items that are fashionable actually make you unattractive to men. Just remember that when you're following fashion, you're dressing to impress other women, not men. Most straight guys are completely oblivious to such trends and the effort is lost upon them. As long as your outfit emphasizes your best features and makes you look alluring, he's satisfied.

Coco Chanel, the venerable fashion icon once said memorably, "Elegance is not buying a new dress." In the end, fashion is often about conforming and doing so quickly. However, you are *not* a conformist. You are an *original* – a one-of-a-kind, unprecedented event in the history of the world. I'm not just saying this to make you feel good – it's an absolute fact. And a large part of your beauty and attractiveness come from your uniqueness as a woman. Be the exception, for that is what makes you exceptional.

Television shows. TV shows are advertisements for advertisements. Once again, the advertisements are like a pesky relative: they tell you sweetly but emphatically, over and over, that you are inadequate. Luckily, you can get rid of the ads much more easily than the relative: simply refuse to watch them.

The average American watches over 4 hours of TV a day. At 15 minutes of ads per hour and 30 seconds per ad, that's about 120 times a day somebody telling you that you need to buy stuff to be adequate. Now don't get me wrong – there have been some excellent shows on television from time to time, and plenty of what's on TV is educational. But there's more 'good' TV programming in a week these days than waking hours in three years of your life. Even in the best-case scenario, watching a minute of TV is a minute spent watching a facsimile of life versus living it. This is the difference between reading about weddings and having one for yourself, the difference between a picture of a strawberry and an actual, red, juicy, delicious fruit you can touch, smell and taste – the difference between the map and the territory.

One could argue that the real substance of life is companionship and connection to other people, and a few times a woman I wanted to spend time with refused or postponed my company because of a television show. Although the behavior is not unusual, passing me over for a TV show is not a good way to make me feel special. If you make it clear to a man that you prefer a TV show to his company, he's likely to accept that at face value and move on.

News media. The ancient Romans had a saying: *sub sole nihil novum* – nothing new under the sun. Whatever a newspaper and radio show can report to you – floods, earthquakes, bombs, wars, treaties, marriages, depressions, celebrations – has happened before. There's nothing *new* about news.

And whose news is it anyway? The media know that bad news tends to sell better than good news – "If it bleeds, it leads" – due to our evolutionarily-designed tendency to want to know about risk so we can avoid it. As such, papers and news shows tend to be a concentrated slug of the collected misfortunes of the world. To maintain a powerfully positive outlook on the world in the face of this hail of negativity is a challenge indeed – akin to staying dry in a rainstorm without an umbrella. Since you tend to get what you focus on, you may wish to consider letting into your psyche only that which is enlightening and uplifting to your spirit – the kind of information that you would *want* to focus on.

This is not a call to provincialism and small-mindedness, and many people need to keep up with the news as part of their work. In fact, there are publications (I'm fond of *The Economist*) that keep you abreast of the planet in a cogent way that is informative without being sensationalistic or containing ads saying you're inadequate. Awareness is a good thing. However, recognize that a majority of news media are profit-driven and thus do not have your mental well-being in mind. As such, they are more likely to add turmoil and anguish to your life rather than equanimity. Therefore, if it is equanimity you seek, you are better off seeking it elsewhere. Let the news go – you simply don't need it.

This passage from Williamson's *A Woman's Worth* summarizes a lot of the points we just discussed about fashion, pop culture and the media:

> *"The monster's third head is the pop culture we collectively spend billions of dollars supporting each year. It does not support us in return. Most movies do not love us, most advertising does not love us, most of the fashion industry does not love us... Like many embittered wives, we look endlessly for love in places with no capacity to love us back."*

Mirrors. Let me tell you a little story. One of the things I really like about yoga is how it can take you into a deep meditative state through movement. During class, everything that used to be on your mind is gone, replaced with a focus on the here and now – your breathing, your balance, your full presence. A good yoga session takes you out of your head into a zone of no-self.

Well, imagine my surprise when I entered a yoga class one day to find it festooned with mirrors. I had never seen mirrors in a yoga class before, and their presence was positively jarring. Not only did I often find myself focusing on my own image in the mirror, trying to figure out whether I was doing a pose 'right', but I also found myself distracted by the images of other people and comparing myself to them. This defeated the purpose of the class.

Needless to say, I never went back to that class, but it made me realize the power of mirrors to put you into a state of self-judgment. When you have a bunch of mirrors around the house, you have no choice but to look at them. And what do you do when you look at them? You *evaluate* yourself. How do I look? How's my makeup, hair, dress? Is my butt too big? Even if you have only three mirrors in your home and you walk by them ten times a day, that's *thirty times* you're assessing that butt in a day.

The practice of embodying the goddess is about allowing your inner beauty to shine. Evaluating your outer appearances hinders that process. So consciously decide to have few mirrors in your household. The one in the bathroom plus another full-length one in a discreet location – preferably also in the bathroom – are plenty.

Bathroom scales. The surface mind is fascinated by measurement. It constantly wants to size a thing up, quantify it, put a number on it, as if by doing so it can understand it. It's interesting that the Buddhist term for illusion – *maya* – comes from the Sanskrit root *matr*, meaning measurement, from which we get words like *meter* and *measure*.

In fact, measurement is an act of illusion. Try this: convert your weight to metric if you use pounds (divide by 2.2) or to pounds if you use metric (multiply by 2.2). So if you're 60kg, now you're 132lb, and vice versa. Notice how you now have no idea whether this is a lot or a little – the number has now become meaningless to you.

Allow me to suggest that the number was meaningless all along and that you're much better off not knowing it at all. Does it really matter to you how much the gravitational field of Planet Earth pulls on your body?

Once again, we have an instrument of judgment. Unless you're a wrestler, boxer or rower and need to make weight for competition, the only reason to weigh yourself is to judge yourself. And stepping on the scale every day is just a crazy-making practice that detracts from your peace, so toss that thing out the window already.

The simple truth is this: when you feel good, you look good. If you don't feel good, you won't look good, regardless of how much you weigh. A little machine that makes you feel bad is clearly not going to help the situation, so you're better off not having one in the household and not stepping on one at the gym, even out of curiosity.

When you feel good, you look good.

Take control of your beliefs

Beliefs are completely hidden from view but determine your behavior. Useful, effective beliefs cost the same as bad ones, so why not use the ones that serve you best? Since no one has access to your beliefs but yourself, feel free to play with them. Pick outrageous, ostentatious, grandiose ones, even if they initially don't seem to resonate with your personality. Think of them as a strategy. If they give you good results, keep them. If not, try new ones until you get the results you want.

Beliefs determine the range of your existence and the limits of your performance. Before you can accomplish something, you must believe that it can be done. Most beliefs that we have regarding our world and our abilities are products of accident or childhood indoctrination by parents or peers. Some of these beliefs still serve us well. But, as almost all of them were patterns laid down accidentally (as opposed to deliberately), many do not. In this chapter, we invite you to take control of your own beliefs and deliberately instill ones that serve you in your goals in the most effective manner possible. Feel free to expand on the ones presented here, or to come up with brand new ones that suit you even better. As for the old beliefs – do not give them too much heed any more. The more energy you focus on the new, more effective, more fun beliefs, the more the brain will automatically allow the tired old beliefs to wither on their own.

This chapter has two parts to it: *content* and *process*. First, we will make suggestions for new beliefs to make you more powerful and effective. Then we will give you methods for instilling those beliefs so that they become a part of your everyday mental makeup.

Exercise 8. Experience how beliefs set the limits of your behavior

Stand up and hold your arms out horizontally. Now twist around in a counterclockwise direction until you can't twist any further. Note exactly how far you have twisted by remembering where your right middle finger is pointing.

Now untwist your body, stand straight, close your eyes and take a deep breath. In your mind's eye, imagine yourself twisting again with your arms outstretched, only this time imagine that you continue to twist, all the way around, 360 degrees, and then one more time, as if your waist was a swivel and you could keep on doing this for three, four full turns.

Now open your eyes again and hold your arms out, and twist again until you can twist no further. Notice how far you have turned. Is it further than before or less? By how much? What is different this time?

Global beliefs

These are global beliefs about how the world works. They are the underpinning of the Taoist way of thinking. Take these to heart, and everything else in the course will follow and flow effortlessly.

1. I believe in the abundance of the universe. Look around you. There is matter, substance, stuff. It is everywhere. There is no vacuum, no void, no antimatter, no non-being – only being. There are over 6.2 billion people on earth, half of whom are of the opposite sex, a good number of whom would make a suitable companion – millions upon millions of possibilities. Even if you eliminate all of those who are of an unsuitable age, station or language such that only one hundredth of one percent of them remain, there are

30,000 left – more men than you could date in a thousand lifetimes.

So relax. Expand your mind to wealth-consciousness and the abundance of possibility, and notice how that brings a calmer, more joyous and more powerful demeanor to you. If you know that the store will always have an unlimited supply of cereal for you, would you ever get anxious about running out? Become aware of your prior patterns of poverty-consciousness, and deliberately replace them with wealth-consciousness. Poverty-consciousness leads to a perception of lack of choice, which leads to being desperate or stuck: "I'll never find another one like him again." Consciously choose wealth-consciousness, and know in your heart of hearts that whatever it was, there's more where that came from. Do that *especially* when all signs seem to point to the contrary. Abundance is simply the way of the universe. If this is the only thing you take away from this course, this book will have been a success.

2. The world is a reflection of me.

If you encounter the world with the attitude of 'Give me', then the world will respond in kind: 'Give me.' If you meet the world with the attitude 'How can I serve,' then the world will respond likewise: 'How can I serve?'

Through this subtle but powerful mental shift, you have in effect turned the world into your most reliable partner. The Hindus call it *karma*: in essence, you get back out of the world what you put into it. Put in positivity and abundance, and that's what you get back. Put in neediness and negativity, and that's exactly what you get back, too. A simple way of thinking about this is that you can't give what you don't have. So if you're giving away friendship, love, and positivity, that means you must have a lot more of it in store.

Since the choice is yours, may I suggest that you believe that the world truly reflects you and bring an attitude of serving and sharing to whatever you do, and watch the miracles that follow.

3. The world is complete exactly as it is, and I am grateful for it. My definition of pain is 'wishing the world to be different than it is.' In metaphysical terms, asking the world to be different (e.g. asking for something in your life) does not serve you because it affirms to the world the lack of that something in your life. If the world is a reflection of you, then it's going to come right back to you and say, "You're absolutely right; that's lacking from your life." So affirming the lack of something has the effect of driving it further away.

But if we still want such things as companionship, intimacy, and sex, how do we approach them if not with desire? The solution is to replace desire with *gratitude* – and, by extension, hope with *positive expectation*. Hope is needy; positive expectation is affirming. When you have gratitude for something, you are accepting its presence in your life and affirming it to the world. In return, the world will do the same and manifest that object in your life.

So you say, "Thank you, world, for bringing so many strong, handsome, intelligent, caring men into my life" – even if you're on the island of the Amazons with no man in sight for hundreds of miles and you haven't had a date for months. And the world will say, "Why yes, you're quite welcome," and good things will happen.

Personal Beliefs

1. Upholding my own importance is a waste of energy.
People expend most of their energy to prove to others that

they are important, cool and therefore worthy of love and admiration. Since this feeding of the ego rarely enhances any kind of real connection or love, the energy is wholly wasted. Relinquishing the need to uphold your own importance frees up an enormous amount of energy towards useful action, harnessing your personal power and catching a glimpse of the true majesty of the universe. All that freed-up energy can now serve you to observe and act more effectively.

> *Most of our energy goes into upholding our own importance ...If we were capable of losing some of that importance, two extraordinary things would happen to us. One, we would free our energy of trying to maintain the illusory idea of our grandeur; and two, we would provide ourselves with enough energy to ... catch a glimpse of the actual grandeur of the universe.*
>
> – *Carlos Castañeda,* The Art of Dreaming

Perhaps now is a good time to do Exercise 9, the Ultimate Freedom Exercise, so you can really feel this concept in your bones:

Exercise 9. The Ultimate Freedom Exercise
Think of your day yesterday, and remember the instances in which you did something to uphold your own importance. Did you belittle someone to prop yourself up? Did you get angry at someone or something? Did you brag, complain, or defend yourself? Become more and more aware of these behaviors on a daily basis, and recognize their folly. And when you recognize their folly, smile and find something to be grateful about – for example, the ability to smile and laugh at yourself. With conscious practice, these behaviors will fall away like dead leaves, leaving you more empowered and free.

---

2. I am complete and beautiful exactly as I am. This belief is corollary to the one mentioned previously about accepting the world (since you are, after all, part of the world). But it deserves special emphasis, because it would seem that fully accepting yourself is not consistent with reading a self-improvement book.

This is not necessarily the case. What this belief emphasizes is that, at any point in your life, you are fully accepting of who you are *right at that moment*. It's not as if right now you're not okay, and there is some point at which you will be okay. You are okay at every point in the process, because you are a creature of never-ending growth and improvement. There is no endpoint, because the only endpoint is now, and there is no time when it is not now.

So be comfortable in your skin *always*; it is the most fundamental aspect of attractiveness. And although you may just be the seedling for a great redwood now, you are still that big tree in essence, at every point along the way. It's just that you keep on growing. And just as the redwood needs water and nutrients to grow, so do you – and you're doing that right now, feeding yourself with the mental nutrients of this book.

> *...The giant pine tree*
> *grows from a tiny sprout.*
> *The journey of a thousand miles*
> *starts from beneath your feet.*
>
> – *Lao Tzu*, Tao Te Ching, *Ch. 64*

A great part of this belief is accepting what you may perceive as faults. No one brings home a perfect report card and neither will you. Human imperfection is not a bug – it's a feature. So let go of that false need. Perfectionism is just another form of self-pity and low esteem. Throw it aside. Relax and realize that everyone has experienced loneliness and failure at some point, so it's normal. Be comfortable in your own skin. Which brings us to the next belief:

3. Being with quality men is my birthright as a woman.
Whether you like it or not, nature has designed you to reproduce. That's what we're here to do on earth. So acknowledge your sexuality, embrace it, and bring its power into your service.

4. I provide the best experience a man could possibly have.
Perhaps you think this particular belief a bit outlandish and not an exact fit for your personality. If that is the case, good: this means we are running up against tired old beliefs that need replacement. Remember: we don't care as much about the absolute truth value of a belief as much as we do about its usefulness.

Right now, chances are that the old belief expresses itself through this whiny voice in the back of your head saying, "Well, *maybe* I'm kind of fun to be around." The fact is that neither your version nor this new version of the belief can be proven or disproven, so why not utilize the belief that will *serve you best.*

Additionally, I want you to really think that you provide the *best* experience, not just a good one. That way, when another woman comes along to chat up the object of your affection, you won't think, "Well, I'm good but she's probably more interesting, or better-looking, so I'll just let her have him." No! The fact is, *there's no way for you to know that.* And when in doubt, might as well assume that you have the upper hand.

The beliefs that last longest are those that have strong support not just in your head but also in the real world. So as you go through this book and incorporate its principles into your life, you will give this and other beliefs strong legs to stand upon.

5. *I am the more important person in the relationship.*
Do you remember the safety announcement that we all ignore at the beginning of an airplane flight? It says that in the case of a drop in cabin pressure, oxygen masks will automatically fall from the ceiling. And if you're with a child, put on your *own* mask first, *then* attend to the child. The reasoning is that if you do it the other way around, both of you are likely to perish, which makes for an unhappy ending. This book is about happy endings, so please do yourself a favor and take care of you first.

This particular belief is not about selfishness but rather about practicality. If there are two people in a relationship, then you have a choice of either making your needs or his more important. If you choose yourself, then you more or less know what you want, and you can handle that. On the other hand, if you make your companion the most important person in the relationship, then you have to *figure out* what he wants. You can do this by asking, or by guessing. If you guess, you're very likely to get it wrong (trust me on this). And if you ask, you're *still* likely to get it wrong, since people are notoriously inaccurate in reporting their unconscious needs and desires at a conscious level.

So your best solution is to stick with what you know, i.e. what *you* want in the relationship, and take care of that first while remaining your kind and considerate self.

This belief applies as soon as you have a relationship with someone, and that happens as soon as you start to relate to someone, i.e. at the moment you say 'Hi.' Start by knowing your truth.

*6. I am **inherently desirable.*** There are people who don't like champagne. Is that the champagne's fault? Does it make the champagne bad? Similarly, you are desirable. Your company is something that all sensible people should seek out. There will be some people who don't quite perceive that yet, and that's okay. That does not change your intrinsic nature which is desirable.

The process of belief

The foregoing nine principles were the *content* of your beliefs. Nine is about the right number because the conscious mind can attend to 7 ± 2 items at a time. For these to affect your life and bring you closer to fulfillment, you must internalize them such that they become a part of your everyday mental makeup.

For that, you need *processes* for internalizing and instilling beliefs. In my experience, one of the most powerful techniques for creating new beliefs and behavior patterns is hypnosis. As a scientist and skeptic who once sat in on a clinical hypnosis class in medical school to heckle it, I have become more and more convinced of the power of hypnosis to effect lasting change and create new beliefs.

Hypnosis works best when done by an expert who custom designs a session for you. As this option may be costly or not available to most people, I have created audio files of hypnotic scripts relating to the material in *The Tao of Dating*.

The next best thing is self-hypnosis. A reasonably good primer on this is *Hypnosis for Change*. More advanced techniques can be found in *NLP: The New Technology of Achievement*. In the meantime, the following three techniques are easy to implement and require minimal effort and time commitment. These are the three that personal development expert Brian Tracy recommends for himself and his students in *Maximum Achievement* and the companion audio course, *The Psychology of Achievement.*

Affirmations. Tracy speaks of the law of subconscious activity: whatever the conscious mind accepts and believes, the unconscious mind immediately puts into effect. So for affirmations to be effective, they must speak the language of the unconscious mind. This means they must have the three P's: they must be *positive*, they must be *personal*, and they must be *present-tense.* As it turns out, the unconscious cannot process a negative. For example, if I told you, "Don't imagine a pink polka-dotted elephant running down the highway," what happens? Did you just visualize the elephant? Exactly. So you must tell the unconscious what you *want* it to do, not what you don't. Tell it, "I am incredibly good with men" as opposed to "I don't want to screw this up again."

The unconscious also tends to be better at accepting statements in the present tense and first-person singular. Say "I am successful" instead of "You will be successful." Writing affirmations every morning in the first minutes after you get up has the magical effect of hard-wiring them into your brain. Make your list of affirmations (perhaps some derived from the beliefs and attitudes we explore here in *The Tao of Dating*) and commit to writing them down in the morning for 90 days. Brian Tracy writes down his goals and affirmations *every single morning,* and he's been doing it for decades, and even though he's a guy, his method may very well work for you, too. It's free to try.

Visualization. See a clear, precise picture of your ideal result. The mind cannot distinguish between what is real and what is vividly imagined. Add in all five senses. Go back to Exercise 4 for an example of this technique. You can attain the picture of whatever you can hold in your mind on a sustained basis.

Acting the part. Some people call this technique *faking it until you make it*. The fact is that beliefs and behaviors are a two-way street: one can create the other. Every time you do something you didn't think you could, your beliefs expand. As your beliefs expand, so does your envelope of behavior.

Sometimes behaviors can create new global beliefs. For example, when you jump out of a plane or walk on hot coals and had never imagined that you could, you may come back from that experience with the feeling that a lot of limitation has been removed from your life. In the case of dating, you may want to act the part that you are incredibly good at meeting and attracting men. Do it as a joke first, and notice any changes over time.

Remember that if you feel that you're not good with men now, it's probably because you pretended that you weren't good with them long enough to turn that into a belief. The good news is that you can use the same process to your advantage and replace that useless belief with a more useful one. You are what you pretend to be, so pretend to be the best you can be.

Chapter 7. Attitudes

The six rules of attitude

Attitudes are the next phase in our movement from the more hidden aspects of personal power to the more manifest. Attitudes are somewhat more overt than beliefs, but still mostly hidden from view.

There are two powerful ways of expressing attitudes. The first is to articulate them as *rules*. Keeping the rules in mind creates the right behaviors which lead to the right results. The other is to think of them as behavioral modes, or *roles* to play. The role has the attitude built in. By naturally falling into that role, you have no choice but to manifest the behaviors that go along with it. Here are the rules:

1. I will not give excess importance to what anyone else thinks or says. This rule is about having an internal frame of reference. Many women try to behave in a way to conform to what a man (or peer) may think. "Will he like this dress? Does he think I look good?" This is a waste of time and a squandering of your personal power. You have no idea what he is thinking, and even if you did, it's a poor guide for your behavior. Much better to know what *you* want, and have him wonder what you think of *him* (which most men are doing anyway). Always assume the position of the buyer.

One of the *Four Agreements* from Toltec spiritual teacher Don Miguel Ruiz's book of the same name is to take nothing personally. It's one of the best pieces of advice I've ever received, and a great way to articulate this rule.

Words can also be deceptive, so be careful about how much importance you place on them. How many times have you heard 'Yeah, sure' when it meant 'No', and how many times have you heard 'I don't think so' only to find out later that it meant 'Well I wasn't sure then but may I have some more now'? This happens over and over again, so it's important to have a more reliable signal than speech. Which brings us to the next rule.

2. I will cue my behavior to what he does, not what he says. Everybody, male or female, needs companionship and likes to have fun, but men and women have been trained to be coy. So we use words as instruments of obfuscation instead of clarification. So in a social interaction, watch him like a hawk. Not only is it flattering to pay him attention, but the information you glean will be invaluable.

So watch for mismatches in his speech and behavior. Is he saying he's not really interested in a relationship while hovering around you the whole time? Does he send you a seemingly bland email the day right after meeting you? Does he say he'd really like to go out with you but in a flat, unenthusiastic monotone?

Pay attention here to the *meta-communication*, not to the content of the communication. For example, if a man calls you five times to tell you he's not interested, then he's *communicating* lack of interest. However, his action – calling you five times – is the *meta-communication*, which says unmistakably that he *is* interested. Conversely, if he calls you once every two months to tell you he misses you terribly (and he lives ten blocks away), then he's really saying he's not that interested.

Also, nonverbal behavior is much harder to fake than verbal pronouncement, so treat the information you get from nonverbal behavior as gold. Is his body turned towards you? Is he leaning towards you or away from you in the conversation? Is he paying attention to you or are his eyes darting around? We'll go into more detail about nonverbal communication in a later section.

3. I will positively reinforce the behaviors that I like in others and neglect the behaviors that I don't like. In behavioral psychology, a reinforcer is something that increases the likelihood of a behavior happening in the future (see *Don't Shoot the Dog* by Karen Pryor). Animal trainers use food rewards to train dolphins, dogs, primates, etc. Luckily, people are much smarter than animals, so you don't need to carry a cod or banana to parties to implement this rule. For people, *praise* and *attention* work just as well. Conveniently, they can also be used immediately after or during the desirable behavior, which is the way a positive reinforcer is most effective.

For example, if he gets you a drink or holds your seat for you, look directly into his eyes and enthusiastically say, "Thank you SO much, that was so sweet of you." For behaviors that you'd like to see less of, withdraw your attention: look to the side, look bored, or turn your body away from him. This is the opposite of getting angry: anger is an unmistakable sign of *attention* and therefore another positive reinforcer. The law of extinction says that a behavior that is not positively reinforced will decay and disappear over time, so just coolly ignore what you *don't* like while making a big fuss about the things he does that you *do* like.

4. I'm not attached to any particular result, so I will flirt with him because it's fun. If you were to remember just one rule when you're going out into social situations, it should be this one. It embodies two key principles: the mindset that you are the prize, and an attitude of detachment. Being desireless and detached from results embodies the essence of Taoist thinking and is the key to effective action. We will go into more detail on tantalizing and flirting in later chapters.

5. I am the only person allowed to assess my success or failure. For better or for worse, rejection hurts, and this pain seems to have been embedded deep into the tribal mind of *Homo sapiens*. Fear of rejection gets in the way of many a woman's romantic success, so we should do something to handle it more effectively. But how do you know when you have been rejected? Where is that rule written?

Well, it's not written anywhere, and even now, if I were to ask you to state explicitly what constitutes rejection, you wouldn't know. Are you rejected if he doesn't return your phone call? If he doesn't show up for a date? What if he really liked you and was too shy to call back? What if he would have been really terrible for you and did you a huge favor by staying out of your life?

What I suggest here is that you craft your personal rule for rejection, and do it in a way such that it's effectively impossible to be rejected. My personal rule for rejection is: "I know I have been rejected when someone proves unequivocally that I have behaved in a malicious way." And since I generally don't behave maliciously, it's rare for me to ever feel rejected. We will go through this exercise in detail in Chapter 9.

On a more metaphysical note, if you have a habit of self-deprecation, stop it. Now. There are enough forces in the world trying to bring you down, and they don't need your help. Be your own best advocate. Build yourself up instead of bringing yourself down; err on the side of pride if you must. Which brings us to the next rule.

6. I will always leave him wanting more. Let's say you were at a theater watching a movie preview, and the preview had all the highlights of the movie. It told you what happens in the beginning, in the middle, and how the movie ends. How compelled would you be to see that movie now? Probably not very.

Similarly, in your interactions with men, you don't want to give away the store. You want to give a preview, a taste of who you are, with the implication that there's a lot more left. Don't tell them too much about your job, your background, or where you're from. Think appetizers, not full courses. The rule applies to physical interactions as well as information. For example, if you can give excellent hand massages, just do part of one hand, then stop, and move on to something else. If you're kissing him, be the first to stop. We'll cover this topic more extensively in Chapter 11.

Your attitude towards your body

Do you like your body? Do you *love* your body? We're all built a certain way, and there's not a whole lot we can do about that. Sure, you can put on makeup, or maybe exercise a little more, but the basics are here to stay.

As I've said before, pain is wishing the world to be different than it is. Your body is part of the world, so you can either fight a futile fight against the way it is, or accept and appreciate it. Here are two suggestions for doing that.

Inhabit your body. At first glance, that may seem like a strange thing to say – how can you *not* inhabit your body? And yet, too many people go about their days filtering out the body, oblivious to its signals, its needs, treating it like some kind of car made of flesh and bone – wash it now, fuel it then, repair it sometime. No! Your body is not the *vehicle* for you – it *is* you. When you speak of the hair, the butt, the belly, the thighs in the same way you say *the coffee table* and *the car*, you objectify your body and distance yourself from it.

When you fully inhabit your body, you start to appreciate it. When you appreciate it, you start to love it. And the more you love your body, the more you love *you*, the more attractive you become.

Emphasize your strengths. No one woman has a monopoly on beauty, and even the prettiest women in the world perceive themselves as having so-called flaws. Everyone has strengths and weaknesses when it comes to appearance. So play to your strengths. Do you have big, beautiful eyes that everyone compliments? Emphasize them. Great hourglass figure? Wear a dress that flatters it. Nice legs? Wear an outfit that presents them well.

Note that men will appreciate you for what you have to offer, not what you don't. So highlight your strengths in the appearance department, don't worry about the rest, and you'll draw plenty of appreciative men to you.

Exercise 10. Accepting and appreciating your body

Find a quiet place where you can concentrate for the next few minutes without any interruptions. Now I invite you to relax... and imagine the time when you were a single cell... just one little tiny cell. This cell divided into two, then four, then eight, then sixteen, then 32. And it kept on dividing, until there were thousands of cells... millions... then billions... then trillions. These cells ordered themselves into muscles to move you, bone to support you, digestive tract to feed you, blood to carry oxygen and nutrients everywhere, kidneys to clean your blood, brain cells to run the whole show. And these trillions of cells all worked together in perfect unison, for years and years, all without any interference from your conscious mind. It's really mind-boggling and a complete miracle that we exist at all. So take a moment now to marvel at this magnificent machine that is you, and give it some deep gratitude.

Every day your body keeps you healthy and alive by fending off billions of infectious agents, by extracting nutrients from the food you eat, by filtering your blood of waste products. So just do a quick scan of your body from toe to head, and as your attention passes over each body part, thank it for all that it has done for you and is doing for you now. Accept your body for the miracle that it is, and appreciate it for the gift that you are.

Love your body now

The following is one of the best pieces I have read on relating to one's body in a healthy way. My good friend Christine Mason McCaull wrote it. She is a truly remarkable woman: entrepreneur, CEO, yoga teacher, artist, environmentalist, writer, wife, and mother of four amazing children. Many of my female friends have found this piece useful, and it's so eloquent and empowering that I really can't improve upon it. She's been kind enough to allow me to include it in *The Tao of Dating*, so I hope you find it useful:

Wherever you are, love your body as it is right now. I mean now, not when it achieves some desired future state or as it was at a reminisced point of peak fitness. I mean now, not when it is ailment-free. It's a magnificent machine, and does wonders for you everyday. Maybe it only gets your spirit from the bed to the bathroom, or maybe it allows you to have babies, or peel a banana or walk to the store or dance Swan Lake or hold a handstand. Whether it is fat or tall or small or imbalanced or polished or bearded or wispy or unpredictable – just love it for what it does for you. Appreciate all the elements and miracles that allow you to live – strong legs, ample hips, the crook of the elbow. The fullness of the heart-beating, veins-throbbing, stomach-growling you!

Decommoditize yourself. Your body may be valued in the abstract by the culture at large for its sexuality, its reproductive and productive capacity, its creative capacity – or any number of other things. Don't allow yourself to be commoditized! There is no cookie-cutter beauty, sexuality, age, or attractiveness. These are cultural constructs, and there is no need to accept these constructs or support their ongoing existence. If you were born in a different place and time, the rules would have been different. They are not real!

Plus, realize that a lot of people make money by trying to convince you that you should be different. They take your resources and power by trying to trick you into thinking you will have more resources and power or love by investing in a stereotype of beauty. Imagine what would happen if the scores of hours and all the emotional and intellectual energy that went into counting calories or self-berating actually went into living! Take a cue from artist Stefan Sagmeister, who says: "Trying to look good limits my life." Derive your value from being most fully alive, from the times when you are intimate, compassionate, caring, creative, engaged – not from the outward projection.

Decommoditize others. Stop praising other people for the values of the commodity-body culture, and start calling out those qualities that make them most themselves, approachable, reachable, human! Begin to notice and compliment people when they embody values that are more to the point: for their humor, intelligence, flair, originality, intensity, focus. Tell them "I love it when you smile – you light up the room!" Even better, take the time to pause and look into people's eyes and lift the veil that separates you. Check your own judgment at the door and try to see the person behind the body.

Get real. Look around you at *real* people and *real* bodies of all ages. How does skin age? Joints age? What's genetic? What's diet and habit? What is the range of appearance? How many people do you see that look like the magazines? This is the range and magnificence of humanity and there is no shame in it. Those who would judge have not yet seen this truth. In this context you are but one in 6 billion – and probably not that different from most.

Want to get really real? Go somewhere and be naked, in a non-sexual way. There are hundreds of places where hippies, free spirits, and those that want to be free go and take their clothes off and lay in the sunshine or ride a bike or swim or just enjoy what Benjamin Franklin called "the air bath"– his recommended practice of laying naked in the open air for an hour a day. See people – scrawny, broad, dimpled, pimpled, *beautiful* people from 8 to 108 being naked just because and not judging each other at all... Feel the sun on your breasts and give yourself a love bath. Walk among others similarly attired and 99.8% won't have a thing to say – you are just a body among bodies, free with no shame.

Heal old traumas in the body. All of the violent messages, imagery, dysmorphia, lack of relevant and meaningful comparison points, abuse, injury – let it fall away. Develop a practice of appreciation, gratitude and genuine *feeling* of being in your body – how the breath moves, how the limbs move, and become free. Any combination of awareness, yogic exercise and breathwork will help you let go of those things which don't serve you.

Show your body love through action. When you love someone or something, you start caring for it, you bring it nice things, you polish it, nurture it, do nice things for it. Take it out to play! Let your love for your body come out naturally – not as a compulsive desire to fix something or get somewhere, but lovingly and kindly from a place of joy. Change through effort stemming from joy, not from a desire to get somewhere for any other reason.

Show your love through kind words and appreciation. The same goes for praise and appreciation. Whenever you hear the old tape in your head saying something like "I am so fat!" counteract it with 3 positive mantras: "This body serves me well, and lets me paint. It lets me climb on the roof, and I am damn happy in the sack." Practice self-massage, giving gratitude for all the parts from toe to crown.

Your body is a plaything for the spirit. Even in saying "I am working on myself", you acknowledge the duality of the spirit, the I, the self, as separate from the body. In moments of peak meditation or tantric experience, you can catch a glimpse behind the veil of the body, seeing to the bottomless depths of another person's soul. Your senses allow experience. Imagine your body as a hula hoop swirling around the soul. Enjoy it, marvel at what it can do, how it works; engage it with the world around you in every possible way.

Part III
Do

Chapter 8. Find

Now that we have established the mental framework for fulfillment – the *Be* phase – we can get on with the practical aspects of *The Tao of Dating*: the *Do* phase. A logical sequence for that is to find the man you're interested in, meet him, attract him, and then perpetuate that relationship through time. This sequence is true of a relationship of any duration, from fling to decades-long marriage. Each of the five stages involves a particular skill set. First is the finding.

The good news is that there are over 6.4 billion people on this earth as of the writing of this book, and about half are male. Eliminating all the men who are too old, too young, taken or not your type and assuming that only one tenth of one percent of all men are single and interesting to you leaves you with your pick from among a mere 3.2 *million* men. That means if you met 100 of them every day for the rest of your life, there would be 1.4 million left unmet the day you die. It is estimated that in the U.S. alone, there are 50 million single men. Think abundance – incredible abundance. Eligible men are everywhere.

The other news is that most women do not meet a new man every day, let alone one hundred of them. When you meet new men on a regular basis, your chances of finding one you like improve. An old Persian proverb says, "From you, action; from god, blessings." So take action. And the first step of the action is mental preparation.

So take a moment to look around at all the manufactured objects around you – stapler, computer, desk, building, monument. There is nothing in this world that did not start out as an idea in someone's head before manifesting in the world as a tangible object.

Now, what if that were also true of your ideal companion? What if by taking a minute of your time to imagine him vividly, you doubled your chances of meeting him? It sounds a little farfetched, but what do you have to lose? What if it actually works? What will you gain if it does? What will you lose if it doesn't?

If you're a bit of a skeptic, that's fine. I am, too, so I'll understand if you just want to skip the 'Ideal Man' exercise below. But take a minute and do the exercise preceding it – the famous 'Quarters' exercise of Robert Anton Wilson, first published in his fascinating book *Prometheus Rising* (which remains to this day the most stimulating book I have ever read). Done correctly, the quarters exercise will make you look at the world in a very different way.

Exercise 11. The Quarters Exercise.
Visualize a quarter vividly — shape, size, shininess, texture — and imagine that you are going to find this quarter on the street, on the sidewalk, etc. Then look for the quarter every time you go for a walk, continuing to visualize it vividly. Notice how many quarters you find during the course of the week.

The first time I heard about this exercise, I laughed. But I had nothing to lose, and it seemed like a fun exercise, so I thought, what the hell, let's try it. And then something bizarre happened: quarters started popping up *everywhere*. On the sidewalk. Next to my car. Under the desk. For a week, I almost didn't have to worry about finding quarters for doing the laundry, because *the quarters found me*. When you do this exercise (assuming that you get the same results as I and everyone else I know who's done it), something very unusual happens: *you, too, start to find a lot more quarters*.

Now the question becomes: is it because the quarters were there all along and now you're paying more attention, or is it because the mind is forging new quarters out of sheer nothing? And the follow-up question to that is: does it matter as long as you're finding the quarters you want? After having done the quarters exercise, you may wish to go back to the Ideal Man exercise if you skipped it, because who knows — it just might work the same way. Whether you create him out of sheer nothing or merely start to notice him when you hadn't before, the result will be the same: his presence where there was absence.

You may have already experienced this if you've ever bought a new car. Recently, I purchased a Toyota Prius. Now, before my purchase, I had noticed some of them on the road, not thinking much of them. But now that I was driving one myself, it seemed like the roads were teeming with them. Every other car now seemed to be a Prius. Did a slew of people just suddenly decide to buy Priuses at the exact time I did, or did I just start noticing what was already there right under my nose?

Similarly, the man whom you will date or marry is out there already. He's not going to emerge fully-formed out of the head of some mythological deity, age 30 and gainfully employed – he's been around for a long time. In fact, you may even know him already. Your task is merely to do a better job of noticing him.

Exercise 12. The Ideal Man.
Describe your ideal man in detail. What is he like? Go into as much detail as possible – the way he looks, sounds, feels, smells etc. Go into even greater detail – the way he smiles, the books he reads, the way he talks – and make a vivid mental picture of him, with sight, sound, feeling and even smell.

Now close your eyes and visualize a picture of you and him together, holding hands and gazing into each others' eyes, as if you are already lovers. How do you feel about him? How does he feel about you? Summon the picture and the feeling, and express gratitude for his presence in your life. Keep that picture in your head and fully expect to meet him the next time you go out. Report back on your findings.

The goal of the preceding two exercises is to effect a mental shift in your mindset towards abundance and wealth-consciousness. Let me use another example. Let's say you go to the supermarket because you need some fruit, and you have money in your pocket. Which one of the following describes your mindset when you arrive at the fruit section?

• Case A: "Oh, look, here's the fruit I was looking for. It's here for me and I can have as much as I need, and there's no reason for me to pick anything but the ripest fruit in the best condition."

• Case B: "Oh wow, look at all that beautiful fruit! What an incredible accident! Will I be able to have any? Will they be willing to sell me some? Maybe if I just settle for the unripe or damaged ones they'll give me a little bit."

Chances are your attitude is closer to Case A than to B. And yet, in the relationship marketplace, an overwhelming majority of people approach a social setting with attitude B in place, even though they are in an identical position. Luckily, you can decide to stop this counterproductive thinking *right now* and adopt the abundance mentality.

The world is already your supermarket, and every time you go out, there are attractive men *specifically* there for you to meet. It's almost as if the world has special-ordered them, just for you. You have inexhaustible money in your pocket in the form of your attractive qualities, and therefore you need not settle for anything but what's best for you. Notice that this is not about haughtiness or arrogance. Are you being arrogant when you pick the best fruit and leave the bruised and unripe ones behind, or merely being sensible? Decide to *make this mental shift now*, and notice how dramatically more willing you are to meet men in social situations with this attitude in place.

The three-step process for finding quality men

Now that you have done the mental preparation, it is time for some real-world technique. There are three steps to the *find* process:

1. Figure out what kind of man you'd like to meet.
2. Go to where he is likely to be found.
3. Have a simple plan for opening and continuing an interaction with him.

Step 1: Figure out what you want. You went into this step a little when you did the Ideal Man exercise. Figure out what you're looking for. You're not likely to find coffee beans in the dairy section of the supermarket, and you usually won't find 40-year old physicians in the same place that 19-year old college guys hang out. Knowing what you want makes it easier to spot it when you see it. Being completely open to meeting any man as long as he's attractive will paradoxically diminish your results. You do better when you have specific selection criteria.

Step 2: Go to the source. Now that you've figured out the kind of man you'd like to meet, you need to figure out where to find him and to *go to the source*. Again, the more specific you get, the more likely you are to find him.

For example, let's say you want to find the kind of man who goes running across the Brooklyn Bridge at 5.30 am. Now all you have to do is simply show up at the Brooklyn Bridge at 5.30 am for a week, and you're likely to meet several men who fit that description. If you want to meet a man who likes classical music, go to a chamber concert. If you want to find an artist, go to a gallery opening. If you like tall Dutch men, go to Holland. If you're interested in someone who cooks, go to a cooking class or fancy supermarkets.

Even though this seems utterly obvious, I belabor this point because so many people neglect it. I often hear women complaining that they're not meeting the right kind of man, only to find out that most of their opportunities for social interaction come from bars, nightclubs and the workplace. These are nonspecific, unfiltered venues, and as such there is no compelling reason for the men there to be your type. Get picky, get specific, and go to the source.

Nonspecific venues are, more often than not, a waste of your time when it comes to meeting quality people – and acknowledged as such by members of the opposite sex. That means that even if you do meet the man of your dreams at a bar, he will likely think of you as "that bar babe," with all the lovely attending connotations.

Step 3: *Be prepared.* The most important technique is to *be prepared.* In a world where men are everywhere, you should be prepared to meet them everywhere. Luck is the intersection of opportunity and preparation – "Fortune favors the well-prepared mind," as Louis Pasteur famously remarked. The best way to be prepared is to have a protocol for meeting a man in a given situation, such that you know what to do without hesitation. I will give you two methods for doing that in Chapter 9, "Meet."

Below I have compiled a list of 12 different types of men that you may find attractive, and the likely venues for meeting them. Some of it may seem obvious, and I repeat it because the obvious is what we are most likely to overlook. As you go through this list, you may see opportunities for improving your own 'find' strategy and realize why you haven't been meeting too many artistically-inclined men at the gym or rock-climbing men at church. A big part of this strategy involves getting involved and developing your interests.

Type of man...	Can be found at...
Artistic	art gallery openings, art classes, museum lectures, acting class
Literate	book readings, poetry readings, literature night classes
Cultured	classical concerts, opera, ballet, book readings, gallery openings
Intellectual	university coffee shops, on-campus lectures, bookstores, book readings, book conventions, scientific or philosophical talks
Adventurous & outdoorsy	Sierra Club meetings, scuba classes, motorcycle lessons, rock climbing gyms, adventure outings
Athletic	yoga classes, spin classes, fitness conventions, classes at your local gym, races (runs, triathlons, bike races, etc), running clubs
Spiritual	yoga retreats, special classes at yoga studios, holistic events, Amnesty International meetings, Esalen, Omega Institute
Kind or civic-minded	volunteer organizations
Affluent	dry cleaners, first/business class, the opera, charity events
Particular nationality	the country in question, local events put on by that country's consulate, foreign movies from that country, cultural societies
Particular ethnicity	ethnic neighborhoods, ethnic restaurants, holiday festivals
Single and looking	anyone who is ringless and unattached on Valentine's Day, New Year's Eve, at church or at a wedding

Bars, nightclubs and supermarkets don't do well on the 3 Cs scale (which we're about to discuss), which means that optimally, you should not *plan* to spend time there. However, if you find yourself already in a bar, club or supermarket, by all means use the system. You have nothing to lose, and practice makes perfect.

The three Cs of optimal venues

The laws of physics say that the initial conditions of any event chiefly determine the course of that event. I have found this to be true of dating as well: the conditions in which you initially meet someone have a large bearing upon the subsequent course of that relationship. As such, it's not only important to choose wisely *whom* you meet, but also *where* you meet him. As such, here are three cardinal characteristics that determine whether or not a venue is optimal for meeting men (and by extension, people in general):

Conversation-friendliness: Since men are primarily attracted through the eyes, you have an advantage in a loud venue since they can still see you. However, to evaluate *him*, you want to be able to hear what he has to say, and for the courtship to progress at all, you need to be able to hear one another. So ask yourself whether a particular venue is suitable for carrying on a conversation. Quieter places are generally better. Loud clubs and bars generally are not, but sometimes their quieter patios or balconies can work. Bookstores and coffee shops are much better.

Community: There is pre-existing rapport when some common thread of interest connects a group together. The more specific the thread and the greater effort people have made to come to the venue, the stronger the rapport, and the easier time you will have making contact. Talking to people watching a game at a bar is likely to be a fleeting interaction, whereas the people you meet at a conference in Buenos Aires on emperor penguins may become lifelong friends.

Continuity: Stationary people are easier to meet than those in motion. The longer people tend to stay at a given venue, the easier it is to meet them. Continuity can also develop over longer periods of time. There is built-in familiarity with a man you see three times a week at the gym which makes it easier to meet him.

Apply the 3 Cs to the various places you spend time over the course of a week. Then decide to spend more time at the places that score higher on this scale. Every minute of your life that you spend doing one thing is to the exclusion of doing something else that could be more rewarding. Economists call this *opportunity cost.* You want to minimize your opportunity cost by making sure you spend time in places that optimize your meeting potential. This means fewer bars and nightclubs (low on all three Cs) and more book readings (high on all three), coffee houses, and group events with friends.

On the balance, you are better served by places that facilitate the connection process, not hinder it. Using the foregoing standard, you can assess how worthwhile a given venue is and apportion your time accordingly.

> **Opportunity cost means that every minute you spend doing one thing is to the exclusion of doing something else that could be more rewarding.**

The optimal venues for meeting quality men

One of the most frequent questions I get from women is, "Where are all the good men?" The answer is that the good men, like the good women, are everywhere. However, there are good places to meet these men, and there are even better places to meet them. The best venues are those that score high on the Three Cs scale, because these are the places where you have an opportunity to make an accurate assessment about the men you meet.

Extraordinary results require extraordinary measures. So if some of these places or events seem unfamiliar or beyond your comfort zone, that is a good sign. Remember that in life, *everything* that you want is outside of your comfort zone. Because if something is inside your comfort zone, it's either something you already have or something so trivial as to be undesirable: you don't *want* something you already have. So in order to get what you *want* but don't yet have, you have *no choice* but to venture outside of your comfort zone.

This venturing could be literal, as in going to a new neighborhood or museum, or it could be metaphorical, as in throwing a party at your apartment when you've never done so before. Either way, I encourage you to enjoy the experience of expanding your comfort zone and recognizing that discomfort is often the surest sign of growth.

Everything you *want* is outside of your comfort zone.

The following are some venues that not only score very well on the Three Cs scale, but also have a highly filtered male clientele. While some of them have a male-to-female ratio that may seem undesirable at first glance, remember three things.

First, you would rather be at a place where there are only a few men with lots of potential than in a place where there are many men with little potential (like a sports bar).

Second, with the willingness and ease that you will have in meeting men through the principles of *The Tao of Dating*, you will be far ahead of the women at any venue who are less willing to initiate contact with men. If there is only one man in the room whom you want to meet, you still have to make the effort to meet him, regardless of whether there are zero women in the room or ninety-nine. So if you're the only woman who is willing to put in the effort, it's effectively as if you're alone with the man.

Third, think abundance. There is no competition; there is only opportunity. And there are millions upon millions of men out there, a good number of whom are worthy of your companionship. Remember: you are attending these events because they are intrinsically worthwhile. Going there primarily to meet men is broadcasting to the world that there is something missing from your life. It's not. Your life is complete. At the same time, you are aware of the opportunities for companionship, fun and fulfillment that the world is presenting to you.

One more thing. Some of the venues and events listed below may strike you as infrequent or one-offs, and they are – like plane rides and weddings. But, as Nassim Taleb discusses in his book *The Black Swan*, improbable events often have a disproportionately large impact. So be prepared for them.

That said, let's see where these worthy men can be found:

1) Dinner parties. This is by far the best place you can meet a man. Why? First of all, it scores very highly on the Three Cs. The venue (usually a private residence) is bound to be conversation-friendly; there is continuity in that all of you are spending several hours together; and there is a high degree of community in that all of you were invited to the party and have at least one friend in common. Weddings and the like also fall in this category.

There are many reasons why dinner parties are quite possibly the best way to meet men. First off, the sense of community engendered by the fact that you've all been invited by one person (you or the organizer) enables good conversation. Second, if you are the hostess, it is a fantastic showcase for your talents as an entertainer and cook. Do not underestimate the power of the hostess.

Most importantly, the men at these dinner parties are going to be *networked-in*. This means that they are already embedded within a network of friends and link back to you through that. The importance of this cannot be overestimated. A networked-in man is much less likely to behave poorly than a complete outsider, because he's aware that his actions carry consequences. Moreover, you (or your friend) have hand-picked these men to be present at your party. Most men would travel any distance for a home-cooked meal. Add to that the potential of meeting fabulous single women hand-picked by you, and the invitation becomes practically irresistible.

A dinner party is a deliberate affair requiring planning and effort. But as with all things, you get out of your dating life what you put into it: results are commensurate with effort. Although making a dinner party happen will take time and money, so do all those nights out and all those dinner dates for which you spent time and effort getting ready and showing up. The good news is that a dinner party is bound to give you a much higher return on your investment of time and effort.

A note on weddings: everything that we said about dinner parties is generally true about weddings, too. Add to that the fact that everyone is bound to look their best, and good feelings are running high in the celebratory atmosphere. The high alcohol consumption and vacation mentality tends to jump-start things. Also, beware of the temptation of starting a long-distance relationship with the handsome groomsman. If you want to have a fun little fling, that's fine. But know that thinking that you can perpetuate that into a full-fledged long-distance relationship is more often than not a ticket to frustration, which is the opposite of fulfillment. Just remember that the long-distance caveat applies.

2) Conventions, seminars and fairs. These events all score very high on the Three Cs, especially on the community aspect. If you have all traveled and paid to attend an event, chances are you have a tremendous amount in common already. Because of the intense nature of these events and the fact that you're spending so much time together in a short span, friendship and familiarity can build very quickly, providing a foundation for future interactions. Additionally, the men are more networked in than the average stranger, since you are all bound to be in the same professional field or community of interest.

3) Gallery openings. Every week, local publications like the *LA Weekly* or *Village Voice* (NYC) list several gallery openings ranging from the avant-garde to traditional. These events rate high on all three Cs, are usually free, and often have free drinks and food. Young, intelligent, artistically-inclined men frequent these openings, and discussing the art is a natural way to get the interaction started.

4) *Book readings and lectures.* Intelligent, educated men go where the books are. Get there early and sit next to the guy you'd like to meet. You can also talk to him after the reading, with built-in conversation starters: "What did you think? What brought you to the reading? Have you read other works like this?" Run with it.

5) *Wine tastings.* These events do well on the 3 Cs and attract an affluent, cultured clientele. And if you're into wine yourself, there's no better place to meet a man with similar oenophile tendencies. The atmosphere is generally festive, and the wine presents plenty of pretext for conversation and jollity.

6) *Yoga and pilates classes.* Your intention for coming to class is always to deepen the spirit by exercising the body, so you're not going to class as a social exercise. However, as long as you're already there, it makes sense to make friends with like-minded people who are also there.

Although generally more women than men attend these classes, the men who do attend tend to be spiritually-inclined, emotionally aware, and educated. Because of the silence and discipline involved in a yoga class, it's not an ideal time to meet people *during* class, so show up early and strike up a conversation *before* class.

After class some people tend to be in a rush to get back home and clean up, but it's often a natural segue to go get a casual bite after class at a local eatery. If he has any sense in him, he would rather eat with you than be alone. People tend to frequent the same teachers and time slots; do the same, and you can naturally and easily build a network of yoga friends.

An even better occasion than the yoga class to meet men is the special classes or events held at your local studio.

Almost all yoga studios have classes on special topics which tend to be much more social than regular yoga class.

7) Community service interest groups. Amnesty International and Sierra Club local chapters are good examples. Men who willingly join these groups tend to believe in their causes and as a group tend to be more conscious and spiritually-inclined.

8) Church services. All kinds of people attend church, so it's up to you to select the type of church (or synagogue, or mosque, or non-denominational spiritual gathering space of your choice) that attracts the type of man you're interested in. The main value of a venue like a church is that it creates community and continuity, allowing you to interact casually with potential dating prospects and thereby get a feel for them.

Two places within the church are particularly suitable for meeting men: the bookstore and church-sponsored activities. The community service activities are best, since that's where you're most likely to meet the warm-hearted men.

On the other hand, I would advise you to avoid assiduously any church-related activity with the word 'singles' in it. From my experience, these events have a slight but distinct odor of desperation to them, and the good men avoid them like the plague while the wrong men show up in droves. Incidentally, I have found this to be generally true of *any* singles-oriented event (see below). You have been forewarned.

9) Continuing education. Adult school, church classes — these are all fantastic opportunities. Go to the classes that interest you, not the ones that you think would maximize your potential for meeting men. Remember, you are the furthest thing from desperate. Take the class because it's fun and it'll make you a better person, because what man in his right mind can resist a fun, amazing woman?

10) ***Running and cycling clubs, races.*** Healthy, fit, affluent men with whom you have at least one activity in common will show up at these events. However, beware of the man who spends a majority of his time training (e.g. triathletes). As great as he may be, he probably won't have much time for *you*. Remember that fulfillment is a feeling, not a person, and creating fulfilling feelings for you requires time. Proceed with extreme caution with any man who doesn't possess enough of this essential commodity.

11) ***Long-distance transportation.*** You're stuck on the plane, bus or train anyway, so you might as well make the most of the situation and meet someone interesting. Sit next to him at the gate; that way, after you've already struck up a conversation at the airport, it's only natural for you guys to continue once you're on the plane and rearrange seats if necessary. Phrase your request to sit with him as if he's the one doing *you* a favor – he would be saving you from the potentially smelly and boring person that would otherwise be sitting next to you. Most men will jump at the opportunity to be chivalrous and have good company at the same time.

12) ***Retreats.*** Yoga or any other kind of retreats are amazing places to bond with like-minded individuals. Friendships are forged here with both men and women that last a lifetime.

13) ***Performing arts venues.*** Cultured, educated, affluent men will be found at the theater, the ballet and the symphony. If this is something you're interested in anyway, go to the event. Then find out about their pre-event lectures, wine tastings and such, or strike up a conversation during intermission.

Some not-so-great places to meet men

Although *The Tao of Dating* is mostly about what to *do* as opposed to what *not* to do, I feel it's necessary to cover why certain venues are particularly unsuitable for meeting quality men. Although some meaningful, long-lasting relationships may have very well started in the places I'm about to mention, those are the exceptions that prove the rule. Generally speaking, if you're seeking a fulfilling, long-term relationship, you're better off spending your time at one of the goldmine venues listed above.

Bars and nightclubs. Aside from the fact that they score poorly on the 3 Cs scale, the main thing that will sabotage the potential for meeting a quality man at these venues is that *you* will be different. You will be affected by the loud noise, perceived competition in the form of other women, alcohol, and irritating crowds in a way that makes it more difficult for you to present your best side – or to perceive his. Moreover, even if you meet Mr. Perfect at such a venue, afterwards you may not be able to take him seriously because of the circumstances under which you two met.

Anything advertised as a singles event. For some reason, these events attract the wrong kind of people on a consistent basis: the desperate, the needy, the clueless, and the just plain bizarre. If that's your dish, by all means go. If not, you're often better off staying at home.

Matchmaking services. Some people really like these 'introduction services', and they're generally free (or nearly so) for women to join, and cost a lot of money for men to join. And that's the problem: the asymmetric involvement of money taints the whole process. Add to that the whiff of gold-digging around the whole enterprise, and you have a setup that does not necessarily have your long-term fulfillment in mind.

On the other hand, if you have friends who know you well and *do* have your best interest in mind and simply enjoy connecting interesting people together, by all means be open to their suggestions. That's how some of the best introductions happen.

Long-distance relationships: a brief, biased rant

Let's say you meet a fantastic guy on a vacation trip. You spend several days together, and generally have a wonderful time. In fact, you get along so well that you decide to continue seeing each other after the trip. There's only one issue: he lives in Austin; you live in Los Angeles. Should you continue seeing him or not?

Here's my stance on long-distance relationships: more often than not, they are a setup for disappointment and heartbreak. A long-distance relationship *could* work out – 'working out' meaning that it brings both partners tons of fulfillment over the long-term and maybe ends up in something like marriage. However, it's not *likely* that it will work out. Now my job is to help you find long-term fulfillment – not quick fixes, not the entertainment of your whim, or any kind of longshot that's over 90% likely to bring you more pain than joy. And the rare long-distance relationship that does work out is the exception that proves the rule.

Here's why. Let's go back to the idea of fulfillment-centered dating. *Fulfillment is a feeling, not a person.* And there are many, many persons who could provide that feeling of fulfillment – just as there are several different kinds of food that could fill you without all of them having to be Cherry Garcia ice cream.

Fulfillment is having someone to catch a movie with on a Friday night, someone to dress up with to the opera and snuggle with afterwards, someone to share brunch with on a Sunday morning. For the most part, someone who lives more than 200 miles away from you cannot provide you with those fulfillment feelings, simply due to geographical constraints.

Before we go any further, let me define what I mean by a long-distance relationship. You are in a long-distance relationship if the physical distance or scheduling challenges between you and your partner *preclude spontaneity* and you can see each other less than once a week. 90 miles of distance between you will do that, as well as exceptionally busy schedules. In fact, you may already be in a long-distance relationship with someone in your own city and not know it.

Now let's explore what would happen if, say, you started to date seriously (whatever that means to you) a man who lives more than 200 miles away. First, chances are you would see each other relatively infrequently – two or three times a month. This means that every time you do see each other, it's just like Christmas! You are thrilled to see one another, and it's a highlight reel of fun times.

As great as this sounds, it does not allow for the natural, everyday dynamic between you to develop – the way you would interact if, say, you were married and saw each other on a daily basis. So even though you're having a lot of fun, you effectively know nothing about one another in a domestic arrangement where you see each other regularly.

Second, no man is an island – they all come with their buddies and cronies, as do you. To assess accurately whether you and a given man get along, you need to see him in his natural habitat (and vice versa). In the perpetual first date that is most long-distance relationships, you'll never find out that his friends annoy you to no end and frankly smell funny. Or that his mother hates you. These are useful things to know *before* getting deeply involved with anyone.

Third, an unconscious undercurrent of resentment will develop regardless of how well you get along because of the sheer effort involved in seeing each other. Why couldn't he be closer? If he loves me so much, why can't he just move here? If *you* don't ask that question yourself, your friends will, and they will also resent the fact that he's the cause of your being away for long stretches of time. Moreover, *he* will probably be having similar thoughts.

That said, there are circumstances under which a long-distance relationship could work out. In my observation, two criteria need to be fulfilled. First, there needs to be a definite deadline by which you have both agreed to live in the same town. Second, you both know beyond a shadow of a doubt that you will be together for the long term when you do make the move. In other words, you're already engaged or close to it.

If you're in doubt and still wondering what course of action to take, err on the side of caution. A man who loves you enough *will* offer to move to your city. And if you truly love him, you will ask him to get his own apartment, since that gives the relationship the best chance of success.

Let's examine two case studies, one in which a long-distance relationship worked and another in which it did not. Perhaps you can spot elements in each story that contributed to the success or demise of the relationship.

Case 1: Hillary and Tom.

Hillary and Tom met through Howard, a mutual friend. Tom was Howard's best friend in college, and Hillary had worked with Howard for several months. Howard knew both of them well and thought they would make a good match, both being highly educated, intelligent, level-headed individuals on successful career tracks. Although both Tom and Hillary had many interests and were lots of fun to be around, neither was the partying type. Both came from stable family backgrounds where the parents were married for over 30 years. Tom was 27 and Hillary was 25 when they met.

On their first dates, Tom and Hillary hit it off. At the time, they both lived in Boston. After a year of dating, they were engaged to marry. However, Tom was to leave for the Bay Area in a few months. They decided to stay together even though Tom was moving to the opposite coast, 2600 miles away. Hillary knew she would be done with graduate school in a year and a half, at which point she would get a job in the Bay Area.

Tom and Hillary actually got married before Tom's departure. And I'm thrilled to say that ten years hence, they are still happily married and just had their first child.

Case 2: Kristina and Jeff.

Kristina was a beautiful 37-year old Hungarian émigré who had lived in Los Angeles for 4 years. She moved to Los Angeles after her divorce and decided to start over. Being independent, driven and adventurous, she decided to start her dream business, and after two years of challenges, the business was starting to grow.

At this time, encouraged by a friend, she decided to attend an expensive 5-day motivational seminar in San

Francisco to get her life on track and accelerate her success. At the seminar, she met Jeff, a dashing, independently wealthy American who lived in San Francisco. The seminar was emotionally and physically intense, and they spent almost all their time there together.

After the seminar, they continued seeing each other, sometimes Jeff coming down to LA, other times Kristina flying up to San Francisco. Every time, Jeff would suggest that Kristina leave LA behind and move to San Francisco to live with him. Kristina was wary of abandoning her business, but he told her not to worry – he had plenty of money and was happy to provide for both of them until she found her footing. It seemed like an ideal arrangement. After a few months, Kristina, with some reservations but feeling adventurous and optimistic, gave in to Jeff's blandishments and moved to San Francisco.

It took about two weeks of living together to make both Kristina and Jeff realize that this arrangement was not going to work. They had never lived together in close quarters, and under the pressure of constant daily contact, the magic in their relationship faded. Towards the end, Kristina felt as if she did not know Jeff very well at all. Additionally, independent Kristina did not enjoy being unemployed, dependent and effectively at the mercy of someone else financially. She moved back to Los Angeles, emotionally exhausted and a little disappointed in herself, but glad that she had extricated herself from a bad situation. She only wished that she had not gotten in that situation in the first place.

These are two real examples of what can happen in a long-distance relationship, and perhaps two extremes of the spectrum. All the same, you can recognize the indicators of potential success and failure of a given long-distance relationship from the way the players and stage are set.

Generally speaking, a high-risk scenario is fun in the short term and painful in the long term. A low-risk scenario may be less fun in the short term but a better setup for long-term fulfillment.

Internet dating: perils and opportunities

There are multitudes of books on internet dating on sale today. This is not one of them. However, I would be remiss not to give the internet a mention, since it's such a powerful tool for dating.

As a woman, online dating provides you with a lot of opportunities since you will usually be in the position of the chooser. If men do most of the pursuing in real life, it's even more so online. Also, many men who are too busy (or shy) to go out will have an online presence, expanding the dating pool for you. In turn, by having an online presence, you are allowing access to that discriminating man who can appreciate the rare bird that you are.

On the other hand, when you get a lot of responses online, you also have to sift through a lot of duds – and that's a lot of work. Moreover, when you meet a man off the internet, it usually means that he's not networked in – he's a total stranger. This increases the likelihood that one (or both) parties will engage in socially dubious behavior since accountability is low. If you're venturing into the world of online dating, expect surprises.

The main peril of online dating has to do with its high potential for disappointment, since it upends the natural order of the mating process. Nature has built in our brains highly accurate, discriminating systems for detecting suitable companions. Upon meeting a man in person, you are immediately sizing up his height, weight, shoulder-to-waist ratio, complexion, general symmetry, strength, smell, tone of voice, and thousands of other parameters you're not even aware of at the conscious level. These systems have worked for thousands of years to help you make a good decision regarding his suitability as a mate.

Online, you have access first to a picture and written description, then maybe a disembodied voice over the phone. And then, if things go well, you may meet in person, at which point you know within the first 10 seconds whether things will move forward from that point on. Most of the time, things don't go any further – after all that investment of time and effort and building of expectation. Whereas had you met in person, the first 10 seconds would have been sufficient to make that judgment.

The best way to approach online dating is the way to approach the rest of dating: by taking it lightly. Chapter 55 of the Tao Te Ching says:

> *The Master's power is like this.*
> *She lets all things come and go*
> *Effortlessly, without desire.*
> *She never expects results;*
> *Thus she is never disappointed.*
> *She is never disappointed;*
> *Thus her spirit never grows old.*

Since I don't ever want your spirit to grow old, I encourage you to avoid activities that involve a high risk of disappointment (e.g. online dating). However, if you choose to brave the waters of online dating, here are some pointers from a man who knows what he and other men find appealing online:

Represent yourself accurately. Ensure that everything you say about yourself – height, weight, age, occupation, location, etc – is accurate. A man will only love you for who you are, not who you are not. Any misrepresentations will come to light upon your first meeting, at which point you'll experience an irrecoverable loss of goodwill, regardless of how much rosy prelude you've been through.

Have as many pictures of you as possible, with clear shots of your face and figure. Make sure you play to your strengths (as discussed previously). Get the shots done professionally if at all possible – they will be worth every penny.

There are many men out there who will like you for exactly who you are and the way you look right now. The better an idea they have of how you look, the more likely they are to interact with you. It's obvious when someone's hiding something, and men will run from that.

Be specific about what you want. The more criteria you have for the kind of guy you want (without being hyper-picky), the more likely you are to find him. It also cuts down on the amount of sifting you have to do through the responses, since the right men will self-select. Be especially clear on your deal-breakers such as age, marital status, pets, children, ethnicity, and religious affiliation.

Be relentlessly positive. Mention all the things that you *want*, not the things that you do not. Negativity is as big a turnoff online just as it is in person. Never air complaints.

Play to your strengths. Online you have the extraordinary opportunity to highlight your advantages – both in appearance and aspects of you that are not noticeable at first glance. If you feel as if you're disadvantaged in the looks department (which is almost never true as much as you think), this is where you can talk up your other strengths –

kindness, humor, cooking expertise, ability to knead him into a pliant pile of putty. And if you're already getting too much of the wrong attention because of your appearance, you have a chance to emphasize other parts of you. *How* you attract has everything to do with *what* you attract.

Use social networking tools to find common acquaintances. If you do have friends in common according to a social networking site, then he's more networked in and therefore a safer bet than before. You may even do some due diligence by asking questions from your common acquaintance.

Chapter 9. Meet

To initiate or not to initiate

Approaching an unfamiliar member of the same species is an anxiety-provoking event across the animal kingdom. Add this to the unwritten social edict not to approach men, and it becomes very rare indeed for a woman to say hi to a man first.

It follows that if you are one of those rare women who is willing to initiate contact with a man, then you are in a position to meet many, many appreciative men. Occasionally you will meet the man who does not welcome your approach for whatever reason (in which case it's a good time to remember again the second of the *Four Agreements* of Don Miguel Ruiz: *take nothing personally*). However, the right kind of man – the man with heart and spine who has excellent self-esteem – will always appreciate your approach for many reasons. It demonstrates your courage, strength, independence of spirit – and your good taste in men, since you've chosen him.

Here's the irony: researchers have shown that in the dating arena, women often *are* the initiators of contact – two-thirds of the time (Moore, 1985). It's just that they're doing it unconsciously rather than deliberately, covertly rather than overtly, nonverbally rather than verbally. A casual glance and a smile in the direction of a man, a flipping of the hair, a turning of the body towards him – these are the subtle but unmistakable invitations to the man indicating your openness to interact. (Of course, after you've been married for years, he'll tell the story of how *he* was the one who got it all started – cute.)

Psychologist Monica Moore observed over 200 women at a party and categorized their successful moves to initiate interaction (technically known as their *nonverbal solicitation signals*). She found 52 of them, some of which I list here in order of frequency of occurrence at the party:

> • Smiling at him broadly (most common by a huge margin)
> • Throwing him a short, darting glance
> • Dancing alone to the music
> • Looking straight at him and flipping hair
> • Keeping a fixed gaze on him
> • Looking at him, tossing head, then looking back
> • "Accidentally" brushing up against him
> • Nodding at him
> • Pointing to a chair and inviting him to sit
> • Tilting head and touching exposed neck
> • Licking lips during eye contact
> • Primping while keeping eye contact with him
> • Parading close with exaggerated hip movement

- Asking for his help with something
- Tapping something to get his attention
- Patting his buttocks

What Moore found was that the more frequently a woman signaled, the more likely she was to get a positive outcome. In fact, the frequency of signaling overrode physical attractiveness as a success factor. In other words, a high-signaling woman of average attractiveness was much more likely to be approached than a prettier but low-signaling counterpart.

Use the tiered approach

So let me make this clear: your job in getting the ball rolling is to broadcast receptivity to his approach early and often. Your receptivity is the feminine yin function which allows the masculine yang function of action to manifest. The man's job is to perceive your receptivity signals on his mental radar. In case a man misses these signals, you can escalate the signal from the subtle to the more obvious until he gets it. The *tiered approach* involves simply observing what these signals are, then using them deliberately, progressing from the covert to the overt until you make contact or ascertain a lack of interest.

Here's a suggested sequence for the tiered approach. Feel free to improvise and expand on it, since you are already far better at this than I will ever be. If the first step doesn't yield the results you want, escalate to the next one until you *do* get the results you want. And remember – discovering that the man is a poor fit for you is also a positive result, since it means you can now focus your energies elsewhere:

1) Start by turning your body towards him, especially your knees, and smiling at him broadly. Supplementing this with

mild hair-twirling amplifies the effect. In this day and age, most guys know that hair-twirling = flirtation.

2) Throw occasional glances in his direction without actually making eye contact. If you are in his field of vision and he's even remotely interested, he will notice this.

3) Next level of escalation is to look him directly in the eye. A friendly smile to go along with it is the most inviting. A challenging look – the come hither look, bedroom eyes, whatever you want to call it – may be too much for most men and scare them away. Remember, you just want to get a conversation started, not to have him abduct you to his cave.

4) Next is to initiate conversation. Many women ask, "Well, what do I say to him?", and the simple answer is: *absolutely anything*. When a woman initiates the conversation with a man, a guy instinctively knows she is showing interest, and he *will* pick up that ball and run with it. And if he does not, then clearly he's not the right man. We'll talk about this more in the next section.

5) Touch him 'accidentally'. It's virtually impossible not to get some kind of response out of a man if you bump into him, so if you're bold enough to use this technique, it has a very high success rate.

6) Wave at him, or wave him over. If you're feeling daring, this will get a positive response out of a man if he's interested even in the least.

7) If none of these work, just grab him by the collars and plant a big smooch on his lips. If that still doesn't work,

congratulations – you have done your part. Feel free to focus your attentions elsewhere.

How to help men approach you

In addition to the tiered approach (remember to smile!), here are some guidelines that will enhance your chances of being approached, especially by a Good Guy:

Have a distinguisher. Guys are dying for an excuse to talk to you – so give them one! A distinguisher is simply an item that is likely to get noticed, setting you apart from the crowd. A fancy brooch, a funny t-shirt, a pink ribbon in your hair, a flower above your ear, a fancy gadget, an intriguing book, seed for the pigeons – these are all perfectly legitimate distinguishers. Remember, the distinguisher's supposed to make it easier for a guy to approach, not harder. Accentuating your cleavage may get you noticed more but not approached more. Which brings us to...

Dress to the sevens, not the nines. Dress your sexy best, but not overwhelmingly so. Even confident guys can lose their bearings when overwhelmed with much skin, cleavage and leg. Also, Good Guys tend to be a little intimidated by (and wary of) really glammed-up women, while the players will fearlessly march forward. By dressing to the sevens, you also leave a little room for turning up the dial later when there's a real date.

Go out in groups of three women or less. It takes a particularly courageous man to dive straight into a gaggle of stylish women and just start talking to one of them. Even really outgoing guys get intimidated doing that – it just doesn't look like a welcoming setup. Besides, the more women there are in a group, the less attention any one of them can get. So why willfully reduce your chances? Go out with one or two girlfriends maximum.

Don't go out with guy friends. Unless your guy buddy is an exceptionally adept wingman, I would advise against going out with him with the intention of meeting other men. Especially if he's good-looking. If I see you with a guy, I will assume he is your boyfriend, brother or protector unless proven otherwise. Which means that I'm much more likely to speak to a woman without a bodyguard. If you are going to step out with your guy buddy anyway, make it clear through body language and distance that he's not an impediment to other men's approach.

Situate yourself in an accessible place. Let's say you're in the corner of an art gallery, with your back to the wall, chatting with three of your friends. Under those conditions, it's almost physically impossible for a guy to approach you without being intrusive. Same goes for sitting at tables in clubs, having your back to the men who'd like to meet you, or clinging too tight to the people you came with.

Wear shoes that are comfortable <u>and</u> look good. I know you love your shoes, and they make you feel sexy and empowered – chest forward, butt out, calves flexed, thighs tight, more height. And nobody's asking you to turn into a frump here. But consider this: there's no better way to wipe a smile off your face than having your feet in pain – *all night long*. And a frown on your face just makes it that much harder for a guy to say hi.

With shoes that are killing your feet, you're also robbing yourself of the chance of a dance or walk that could make the evening. Your mobility and flexibility empower you more than 3 inches added to your height and a hobbled gait.

And when you willfully take away your own ability to walk more than three steps, you will most likely irritate even the most gallant of men – trust me on this count.

Uncomfortable shoes, no matter how hot they make you look, tend to take away more options than they give you (and guys couldn't care less what brand they are). And they kind of beat up your body. For an evening, pick shoes that look good *and* feel good.

How to initiate conversations

Remember that *anything* that you say is sufficient to get the ball rolling, so there's no need to get fancy or overly flirtatious here. That way, if you find that you need to end the interaction early, you can do so effortlessly and graciously. Innocent enough topics of conversation that women have used to successfully initiate conversation with yours truly:

1) A comment on an item of clothing (e.g. "Nice ring/hat/shirt, where did you get it", etc). You are a woman, and it's perfectly normal for you to be interested in such things. And if the man has a sense of style, he'll appreciate your compliment and take it from there.

2) Ask him for some kind of help ("Do you know where the bathroom is?", "Could you please hand me a napkin?"). Men are nurturers by instinct, so you are engaging their noblest nature when you ask them for assistance. No man will be able to refuse a simple request like that, and he'll feel six inches taller for having been helpful.

3) Ask him a factual question or for his opinion. Men are vast repositories of mostly useless facts and entirely useless opinions, so this approach has an excellent chance of success.

4) Tell him that he looks familiar and you're wondering where you may have met before. Although this may seem a tad disingenuous if you really haven't seen the fellow before, it's almost never interpreted as such by the man. In the process of figuring out where you have or have not met, you often find that you really do have things in common, and you can take it from there.

The importance of intention

A key aspect of moving with the Tao and having the Tao help you along in your quest is *intention*. Most of the techniques in this book will work regardless of your intention vis-à-vis the men you meet – anywhere from "I want to meet the man I can cherish for the rest of my life" to "I want to have a one-night stand." However, *The Tao of Dating* will work most effectively when you have a strong *positive* intention which incorporates the beliefs we discussed in Chapter 4, the most important of which being "the world is a reflection of me."

So if you approach the dating arena with the attitude "What's in it for me? What can I get out of this?," the world will respond by saying right back to you, "What's in it for me?," and you will encounter scarcity (or meet men who share the 'taking' mindset with you). You will be much more effective if you approach with an attitude of *giving and sharing*: "How can I serve? How can I enrich my environment? How can I bring something to this man's world that was missing before?"

The fact is that you *are* bringing something valuable to a man's life – your warmth, your caring, your wit, your beauty, your interest, your *presence*. You are a woman. Wars have been fought over you, tomes have been written about you, monuments have been built to you. When you truly believe the value of your presence, it becomes very easy to have the positive intent of bringing that value into someone else's life. The more positive your intent, the less energy you have to expend hiding it, and the more energy you free up to be more effective and have more fun.

You may think of the powerful positive intent (PPI) as a noble stance and a way to be good. But that is not necessarily the way of the Tao: the Tao finds all enforced nobility and goodness suspect:

The Master doesn't try to be powerful;
Thus he is truly powerful.
The ordinary man keeps reaching for power;
Thus he never has enough.

The Master does nothing,
Yet he leaves nothing undone.
The ordinary man is always doing things,
Yet many more are left to be done.

The kind man does something,
Yet something remains undone.
The just man does something,
And leaves many things to be done.
The moral man does something,
And when no one responds
He rolls up his sleeves and uses force.

When the Tao is lost, there is goodness.
When goodness is lost, there is morality.
When morality is lost, there is ritual.
Ritual is the husk of true faith,
The beginning of chaos.

                 – *Lao Tzu*, Tao Te Ching, *Ch. 38*

Rather, think of the PPI as another manifestation of enlightened self-interest: this is the way because it is more *effective*. The Tao would much rather have you be effective than good. The following exercise demonstrates how powerful positive intent empowers you.

Exercise 13. Powerful Positive Intent (PPI)

Imagine that you are on a sidewalk and you see an unusually handsome man. You find him very attractive, and would like to speak to him. Notice how you feel about approaching him. Do you go right up and speak to him, or is there some hesitation? Are you certain that he will immediately like you, or is there some doubt? Now imagine that a crazed cyclist is coming behind him and is clearly about to hit him. Now how much hesitation do you have to yell *"Watch out!"* at the top of your lungs and move him out of harm's way? How much doubt do you have? What is different from the first scenario? What if you were to bring the same powerful positive intent as in the second scenario every time you meet a man? How would that change your behavior? How much more effective would you be in your interactions with men?

Below are some more examples of PPI statements from other women who have had some great relationships. Notice how they all have *sharing* as an explicit or implicit theme. Use them as suggestions to craft your own PPI:

"I want to share my joy of life."

"I want to provide the support that allows a man to blossom and grow beyond what even he himself thought possible."

"I want to create a home full of love, abundance and joy with a great partner."
"I love everything about men and want to express my deep appreciation of them."

Exercise 14. Craft your own PPI to act with greater authority and integrity

Write your very own PPI. It should start with "I ...", be brief, and easy to remember. Make it big and bold. Make sure it resonates deeply with who you are and what you believe. Stick a little clause about sharing if you can. You know you have a good one if it leaves the world a better place when applied universally (i.e. it fits Kant's categorical imperative). Remember it every time you are out meeting men – maybe even keep a copy of it in your purse.

From reading the previous chapter, you now have a sense of the kind of man you'd like to meet and where he is likely to be found. But before we go into further detail on where to meet men, we will go over one of the most pivotal concepts in this book: the Pipeline of Abundance. The most important mindset in this book is that of *wealth-consciousness* – noticing the sheer abundance surrounding you at all times. The mental exercises provide the foundation for the mindset; validating it in the real world cements it in, making it permanent.

You validate the mindset by meeting men all the time. The more quality men you know, the more options you will have for dating, and the less hungry (or scarcity-conscious) you will be about them. So celebrate abundance and always welcome new men into your life.

Exercise 15. The Cookies Experiment
Let's say you have twenty cookies right now. Would you give me one if I asked for it? Chances are you would. What if I asked for two? For three? Twenty cookies are far more than you can eat, so unless you're unusually greedy, you would be willing to part with even three. Now let's say for some reason you lose 19 of your cookies and you're left with one. Now how do you feel about giving me that last cookie? How is your attitude different?

The three-man plan

From the cookies experiment, it's easy to see how our behavior changes when confronted with perceived scarcity. The more choices you have, the freer you'll feel. And this bears directly upon your behavior – in the case of the cookies, being generous or stingy, abundance-conscious or scarcity-conscious.

Similarly, in the dating arena, it's important to have options. So I encourage you to be dating at least two, ideally three men at any given time. No, you won't be a slut for doing so. And you don't have to get physically intimate with all three or any of them. But having three men or so in a rotation is great for many reasons.

First of all, dating is a skill that improves with practice. The more men you interact with, the better you understand them, and the better you figure out what matters in a companion. That's fairly invaluable all by itself.

Second, imagine this scenario. You're applying for jobs. You get several interviews, but only one company offers you a position. How much leverage will you have

188

when negotiating your salary? Not much – you're completely at their mercy. Now imagine that you have *three* job offers. How much leverage do you have now? Exactly. Dating more than one man at a time gives you latitude and keeps you from ever feeling needy. Since two is only one step away from desperate, three is the ideal number to keep your attitude self-sufficient and abundant without letting things get too out of hand.

Handling rejection

Fear of rejection is a perennial source of social anxiety for both men and women. What's it good for anyway? Anthropologists hypothesize that our built-in aversion to social rejection has to do with our history as hominids evolving in savannah-dwelling tribes. Over the course of several hundred thousand years, the social unit of the tribe was about 100-150 people, and everyone knew each other (for a fascinating discussion of tribe size and the 'Rule of 150', see Chapter 5 of Malcolm Gladwell's *The Tipping Point*). In such a small social unit, there was a very high premium put on social harmony. As such, social rejection was tantamount to a death sentence, since ejection from the tribe meant a cutting off of resources and reproductive opportunities. The next tribe was usually too far away and unlikely to accept a stranger. Therefore social disharmony was selected against, and social harmonization and rejection avoidance, with their survival advantages, were passed down the generations. This makes most of us scaredy-cats when it comes to dating, even though conditions in our modern metropolises are very different. Luckily, with some insight and practice, you can get rid of this impediment. Here are two suggestions.

Becoming Rejection-Proof I: Re-write your rule

We briefly touched upon this before: how do you know for sure when a given man has rejected you? Is it a particular sequence of words that he says, or some facial gesture of his? Or maybe it's a feeling you get – if so, where does it start? Can you describe it? Most people don't really have a concrete answer to these questions. And each woman I've met can come up with examples of when she *thought* she was being rejected but really wasn't. My point is this: you probably don't have a hard-and-fast rule for knowing when you've been rejected. And usually it has to do with some external factor ("He said this", "He didn't return my phone call") rather than some internal rubric having to do with you.

So may I suggest that *right now* we establish your rule for rejection which establishes when you know beyond doubt that you have been rejected. And since you're the one writing it, may I suggest that you make the rule such that a) *your* behavior decides it, not external events and b) you effectively make it impossible to be rejected.

For example, my personal rule for rejection is this: "I know I am rejected if I know unequivocally that I acted maliciously towards someone." Since I generally don't act maliciously, I have effectively made it impossible for me to reject myself.

Exercise 16. Write your personal rule to make rejection an impossibility
Write your rule for rejection, starting with the statement "I know I am rejected if…". Then put in there the action *you* have to take in order to know that you have been rejected. Feel free to use variations on the example used above.

Becoming Rejection-Proof II: Re-framing

One very useful technique in hypnosis and neuro-linguistic programming (NLP) is *re-framing*. Since we have considerable latitude in interpreting the meaning of events – free to pick positive, neutral or negative ones – we should pick meanings that are most useful to us. The useful interpretations will tend to make us feel better and be more effective, while the negative ones have the opposite effect. And remember – the Tao's pulling for you to be more effective.

For example, you can interpret a police car on the side of the road as "He's there to get me," or "He's there to keep the neighborhood safe", and you will have different feelings associated with each interpretation.

When it comes to dealing with men, if you feel you may have been rejected, instead of thinking "That guy must not really like me" or "I must be an awful person," try thinking this: "I never get rejected – I only find out which men have excellent taste. And if he says no, he has done me a great service by saving me time and effort." Notice how with this re-frame, you can actually *feel good* about rejection and use the event as a positive impetus to meet even better men.

Here's an example of re-framing dealing with a common dating situation: a man takes his sweet time to call you, either after taking your number or after a first date. A neutral interpretation of the situation would be to imagine that he dropped his phone in a bucket of water and lost your number. A negative interpretation would be that he didn't think you had chemistry. A positive interpretation would be that he was so overwhelmed by your charm, elegance and beauty that he's too intimidated to call you.

Each of these three situations have happened to me and probably to many other men, so they're not entirely fictional. Yet notice how your reaction to them is different. So feel free to pick the neutral or positive re-frame henceforth.

The other powerful reframe you can use is to imagine each approach not as an opportunity for success or failure, but as a chance to *see what happens*. Approach the situation not with a do-or-die mentality, but rather with endless curiosity. A time-honored saying in NLP is that there is no failure – only feedback. And since *something* is going to happen 100% of the time, you are *guaranteed* feedback and cannot possibly fail! I find this reframe to be one of the most powerful. It just enlivens the dating process (or anything else in life, for that matter). It provides the motivation to open yourself up to wonder and to imagine what that gift-wrapped box of possibility holds as you just wait to see what happens next. Always remember that dating is supposed to be fun.

Chapter 10. Attract

You have an unfair advantage – use it!

I have good news for you: you are a lucky woman. Why? Because you're a woman! In the mating dance, men are the pursuers and you the pursued. And you already possess *all* the necessary gifts to attract men into your life. In fact, you are custom-made to make pretty much any man fall for you. It's simply a matter of awakening those gifts to bring into your life the kind of man who fulfills you.

The three components of attraction

I like to think of attraction as happening at three levels: that of head, heart and genitals (or mind, spirit and body). These correspond to three chakras, or energy centers, from Hindu philosophy (*ajni, anahata* and *swadisthana,* respectively). Ideally, you would want a man with whom you can connect at the level of all three chakras. Hence, it makes sense to cultivate your attractiveness at each of those levels.

Another reason why it's important to cultivate all three chakras is this: the kind of fish you catch has everything to do with the kind of bait you use. If you use your sensuality and sexuality as bait, you're likely to end up with a man who's interested only in your body. If you primarily connect with men intellectually, you may end up with a guy who's great to talk to but isn't compatible with you physically. And a super-sensitive guy who's all heart may not be all that fun to talk to.

So strike a balance between your head, heart and body and give attention to all three. All great, lasting relationships will have a strong connection at all three levels.

What we will emphasize in this chapter is femininity – how to cultivate the yin aspect (or, if we want to be consistent with our Eastern philosophical systems, the *shakti* energy) at each of those three chakras. Since most of the men you encounter will have a masculine essence, they will be attracted to the feminine in you. The more you practice femininity, the more you will draw men to you like honeybees to a flower.

There lies enormous power in these practices. If you do them well, you will have the capability to entice any number of men out there. However, with power comes responsibility, so remember the principle of enlightened self-interest: what's best for you in the *long term* tends to be the best course of action right now. Becoming the temptress that cuts a mile-wide swath of destruction through the hearts of men will likely cause you much inconvenience in the long run. Have fun, and use your powers judiciously.

If some of these practices seem foreign or too feminine and you'd rather reside more in your masculine essence, consider this. Have you ever met a man who is super-sensitive, indecisive and passive? Essentially, a man who just struck you as really effeminate? How attractive did you find that? How *annoying* did you find that? Rest assured that a man finds an excessively masculine woman just as unappealing. So in your intimate relations with men, go easy on the masculine energy. As Williamson said, major in the feminine and minor in the masculine. We love you because you're a woman, so go ahead and be a woman. We guys think it's kind of hot.

Attract with your physical presence

Men are attracted to your radiance. Now everyone knows radiance when they see it, but what is it exactly? It's difficult to describe. My best explanation is that it's life force itself. People coming out of an exercise class radiate. Kids radiate. Animals in the wild radiate. The kind of radiance you possess as a woman is all of that, and a lot more. It contains a sexual element, a promise of communion, and the very light of god. It is what men crave.

If you wish to be radiant, project *sensuality*. Sensuality means engaging with your senses. Actively see, hear, taste, smell, and most of all, *feel*. When you fully inhabit your body, own your sexuality and feel the full force of your femininity, you radiate. There is nothing more attractive to a man than a woman in full possession of her femininity. Just thinking about it makes them swoon.

You can find entire books and seminars devoted to sensuality. For a quick introduction, I heartily recommend *The Sensuous Woman* by "J". It is a slim volume and very easy to read, and its practices can completely transform your life within the hour or two it takes to read it. Since "J" wrote the book in 1969, some of its references may seem outdated, but the premise is timeless: when you choose to become a sensuous woman, few men can resist you. She has 10 sensuality exercises in that book, and you would do well to practice all ten.

The next exercise is inspired by that book. You can do all of it or as much of it as you have time for. It's one of the most important, transformative exercises in the whole book, so even if you've skipped all the other exercises so far, *do this one.*

Exercise 17. Cultivate your sensuality.
This exercise works best right before going to bed. Make your bed with fresh sheets. Sprinkle it with some perfume or essential oils. Make sure the room is sufficiently warm. Prepare some music that you find soothing and romantic. Turn out the lights and put on some candles.

Now go take a bath (or shower, if you don't have access to a tub). Don't use a washcloth – wash yourself with your bare hands. Do it slowly, and pay close attention to the sensation of your hands on your body.

As you soak in the water, pay attention to everything that you hear, see, feel and smell. How does the water temperature feel on your body? What does the soap smell like? How does the sloshing of the water sound? Really engage with your senses as much as possible. You'll find that this will clear your thoughts and relax you tremendously.

When you feel sufficiently relaxed, get out of the bath and blot yourself dry with a towel, gently, slowly, as if you're a priceless jewel. Now put on the music and get in the fresh sheets (yes, you're still naked). Notice how they feel on your skin and the smell that they have.

Next, close your eyes and pay attention to your breath. Imagine that sensuality and pleasure have a color. What color would that be? Imagine that you're breathing that color into your lungs with each inhalation. With each

---

exhalation, breathe that color into your body, starting with your feet. Breathe two breaths of pleasure into your toes, your sole; then your calves and shins; knees and thighs; buttocks and groin; torso and chest; arms and hands; head and neck. Wiggle each body part a little as you breathe that pleasurable color into it.

If you haven't already put on some music, do so now. Now feel your whole body tingly and energized as a result of breathing into it. Wiggle all your body parts again and start moving to the music. Now rise and dance to the music as if you're Salome dancing for King Herod. If it feels strange to you, then you're doing it right. Close your eyes and imagine that a throng of men are utterly entranced by looking at you. Sway, undulate. Move your hips. Run your fingertips over your skin. Let the music move through you like a river of pleasure as you feel your whole body come alive, inside and out.

When you feel like you are the very shining goddess of sensuality, you can turn off the music, crawl into bed and get some well-deserved, soothing sleep with a big smile on your face.

Have fun while you transform

I wrote this book for a simple reason: I want you to win. I want to see you beaming from ear to ear because you are with the dream guy whose company makes you deliriously happy. I want to give you advantages that put you head and shoulders above all the other women out there who haven't read this book. So have fun doing the practices. You'll get a lot more out of the book that way, and a real shot at transformation.

You bought this book because you wanted change in your life. I absolutely know you can do it. I believe in you. Your sensuality is like any other skill: you get better at it the more you practice. So let's roll up your sleeves and have some fun with this stuff, shall we? Here are some ideas to get you started on your sensuality practice.

Do yoga. I have always said that yoga is the single most transformative practice I have taken up as an adult. It makes your body strong and flexible, it focuses your mind, and it calms your spirit. It also makes you glow. Ever seen a group of yogis coming out of a challenging class? They all look like human beacons.

Of all the forms of exercise I've engaged in, yoga has been the one that has made me most body-aware. It's a whole-body, whole-mind practice. So if you don't already do yoga, give it a try. If you already do yoga, work your way to the most vigorous class and make sure you practice it three times a week; twice at the very minimum. If you don't have a yoga studio nearby, do it at home by following a recorded program. I recommend the work of Baron Baptiste.

If taking yoga classes is simply not in the cards for you, do regular vigorous exercise. Athletes glow with vitality, and vitality is the same as sexiness.

Dance regularly and take dance classes. So much of modern living is sedentary that people forget that the human body is designed to move. There is no better way to reconnect with your sensuality than to dance, since it fully engages all five of your senses and takes you out of your head.

Dancing alone is fantastic, but what can truly amplify your sensuality and femininity is partnered dancing. This type of dancing cultivates the masculine-feminine dynamic as you learn to relax into your partner's lead and really enjoy that.

Specifically feminine forms of dance, such as belly dancing, are also great ways of cultivating feminine sensuality through movement. As a man, I can tell you that the way a skilled belly dancer moves her hips, undulates, shimmies, gazes coyly and uses her whole body as a symphony of sensuality is irresistible. A woman who can move like that has enormous power over men.

Notice that all of these practices are their own reward. Even if taking yoga or dance classes does not bring you a great man, your life will still be richer and more fun because of engaging in them.

Also notice that these practices aren't teaching you anything that you don't already know. They are merely unveiling the sensuality within. A story about the Coen Brothers movie *O Brother, Where Art Thou?* illustrates this point. There's a scene in the movie in which three river-sirens are supposed to tempt the three chain-gang men (played by George Clooney, John Turturro and Tim Nelson). The women asked Joel Coen, the director, what they should do. Joel gave them a two-word instruction: "Beckon them." Apparently, that's all they needed to hear. If you've viewed the scene, the women undulate, soften their gaze, lower their eyes, tilt their necks, look at the men sideways, push forward their chest, touch themselves strategically and do an altogether fine job of beckoning. To see for yourself, you can look up that scene online right now.

Do you know how to beckon a man? Oh yes you do. The more important question is, when was the last time you used that skill? And why so long ago? Use what your mama gave you.

Attract him with your mind

You are a smart woman. How do I know that? Because you bought this book! Kidding aside, I wrote this book specifically for smart women like you. Which is why some of you may find what I'm going to say next a bit challenging.

Remember that attraction is created through *polarity* – when you are the yin to his yang. Therefore one of the most powerful things you can do to attract a man intellectually is to *be receptive*. In other words, draw him out and listen to him. Because heaven knows men like to talk about their interests.

At the same time, a little bit of feistiness can amplify that polarity. Have an opinion! Speak your mind! Ask questions! Intellect and talent in a woman are tremendously attractive – in fact, the most appealing aspect of a woman for most of the smart men I know. So if you're brilliant and have something to say – shine, sister, shine. Challenging a man and asking probing questions is one of the most potent ways of sparking the attraction between you two. When you do this in a playful, non-malicious way, you will be head and shoulders above all the other women. And the smart guys will love you for it.

Well, it sounds like I just gave you two completely conflicting set of instructions. It's all about balance. Be wary of what can happen if you were to find yourself competing with a man intellectually, or talking over him, or challenging him. Because that's when the polarity can get compromised. And if you're completely passive, that's no fun either. The Tao is all about following the middle path. Balance is of the essence.

If sometimes you feel the need to assert yourself to the point that you're trying hard to prove your point with a man, consider this. It all comes down to what you would rather be: cherished or right. If you spar with the man, you may end up being right – and alone. If you'd rather be cherished, then draw him out and listen to him like your life depended on it.

Remember that sometimes it's okay for the two of you to have different opinions. This is what my therapist friend Michelle calls *the art of allowing*. You are allowing the man's opinion to be different from yours. When you *allow* the man to be as he is, you are making a conscious choice and therefore empowering yourself. In turn, you should seek someone who allows you to be as *you* are.

Before we go into the art of listening, a note for the exceptionally smart women out there: never, ever compromise or hide your intelligence for fear of turning off a man who can't handle it. You need to be you, and the world needs to see you shine. So you need to find a man who can appreciate your blazing intellect without being intimidated by it. Although they may be a little tougher to find, there are plenty of brilliant men out there who are looking for someone just like you. Have the patience to find one of them.

The wisdom of paradox

If some of what we have discussed so far seems a bit counterintuitive, that's okay. The wisdom of the Tao is often paradoxical. Just remember to keep an open mind and try everything out to see how well it works for you – without *a priori* judgment as to how things *should* work. Think of it as a one big experiment, without any attachment to results.

When a superior woman hears of the Tao,
She immediately begins to embody it.
When an average woman hears of the Tao,
She half believes it, half doubts it.
When a foolish woman hears of the Tao,

She laughs out loud.
If she didn't laugh,
It wouldn't be the Tao.

Thus it is said:
The path into the light seems dark,
The path forward seems to go back,
The direct path seems long,
True power seems weak,
True purity seems tarnished,
True steadfastness seems changeable,
True clarity seems obscure,
The greatest art seems unsophisticated,
The greatest love seems indifferent,
The greatest wisdom seems childish.

The Tao is nowhere to be found.
Yet it nourishes and completes all things.
    – Lao Tzu, Tao Te Ching, *Ch. 41, transl.*
Stephen Mitchell

For example, the counterintuitive wisdom in what we just discussed is that a mildly contrarian stance – being feisty – can stoke the fires of attraction faster than a blandly acquiescent stance. The scientific explanation behind it is that mild antagonism causes the secretion of adrenaline, which mediates arousal and rapid attraction (Fisher, 2004). I don't necessarily advocate starting a fistfight when you first meet a man (if you do, do me a favor and report back on its effectiveness), but it's a safe bet that a little feistiness will draw him to you more than just being nice.

The Art of Listening and the Magic Question

One of the most powerful actions you can take to spark the attraction between you and a man and distinguish yourself from other women is to listen – *really* listen. Nowadays it seems that hardly anyone can finish a sentence before getting interrupted by friends chiming in with their own thoughts. Not you! You know how to stay completely silent and *just listen* as the man (or anyone else, for that matter) says everything he has to say. Resist the temptation to say "Oh my god, that same thing totally happened to me!" Resist the temptation to insert a witty comment, no matter how appropriate it seems. People are so rarely listened to that if you just do that, the man will think the world of you.

There's an old saying that goes, "Bad conversationalists talk about themselves. Good conversationalists let you talk. Great conversationalists talk about *you*." Turns out the best way to be interesting is to be *interested*, and just let the guy talk. Thus, the hidden benefit of listening is that he'll think you're *really* interesting.

Of course, this listening thing may not come naturally. But neither does championship horseback riding or playing the violin. Dating is like any other skill, and to get good at it, you practice. Learning how to listen well is a skill that will hold you in good stead for the rest of your life, so it's well worth honing.

Exercise 18. Listen.
This is also called the *dyad* exercise. You need a partner to do this one. The exercise is best done in person. Tell your partner that you are going to do an exercise in listening. Now ask your partner "What are you interested in?," and listen to the response. Look your partner directly in the eye and do not say anything until your partner completely stops talking and signals that it's your turn to speak. Then say "Thank

---

> you," and switch roles. Do this for at least three rounds. Notice the urges that come up — to interrupt, to chime in with a thought, to offer a word or a sigh of support — and how it feels to just let them go. After the end of the exercise, ask each other how it felt to be truly listened to.

That's a tremendously useful exercise, and I really encourage you to try it at least once. When you do, you'll realize how rare it is for us to let someone else complete a thought and be completely heard out, and how often our own little ideas pop up and want to interrupt.

If you learn to listen well, I promise you will be head and shoulders above every other woman out there — provided that you incorporate the following additional technique into it. Remember how we said that the great conversationalists talk about *you*? Well, you want to make this conversation about him. The way you do this is with a simple yet infinitely powerful question that you will ask again and again. I will call it the Magic Question:

"What's important to you about that?"

If you detect this to be a fancy way of saying *why*, you are correct — that's exactly what it is. However, *why* sounds a bit confrontational and judgmental — "Well, why'd you do that? Why didn't you do something else?" *What's important to you* sounds a lot softer and is much more likely to get useful information.

The key to doing this process enjoyably and effectively is to ask only questions you're genuinely interested in. This is not a job interview. It's the discovery of another soul — one who could become your lifetime partner! So cultivate a boundless curiosity for people.

Now each time you ask a person the Magic Question, you will get closer to what really matters to him. You are getting closer to his core values – what really motivates him and makes his life meaningful. This has a twofold benefit: he's feeling heard and understood like never before, and therefore will be attracted to you *and* you're getting invaluable information about what he's really made of deep down inside.

When you listen while using the Magic Question, you're employing both your yin and yang energies to create attraction. Your yang energy activate by your engaging with him with questions, which is a form of leading. Your yin powers activate when you listen receptively.

Notice that there is nothing passive about what you are doing here. Taoism has often been accused of passivity, of a go-with-the-flow kind of attitude. This picture is true but incomplete. You are *choosing* to do all these things deliberately, which is the opposite of passivity. And if you think the whole idea of taking on yin energy means more passivity – think again. That listening exercise, when you're supposed to not say anything at all when the other person speaks, may very well be the toughest one in the book. And if yin energy were about passivity and just sitting there, why would we need exercises to practice them?

Yin and yang energy are two aspects of the same energy, like positive and negative charge, or a mountain and its shadow. One is not superior to the other, like one side of the coin is not better than the other. The two energies complement one another to create universal harmony. Flowing with the right energy at the right time gets you where you want to go. Chapter 2 of the *Tao Te Ching* says:

Being and non-being create each other.
Difficult and easy support each other.
Long and short define each other.

High and low depend on each other.
Before and after follow each other.

Therefore the Master
Acts without doing anything
And teaches without saying anything.
Things arise and she lets them come;
Things disappear and she lets them go.
She has but doesn't possess,
Acts but doesn't expect.
When her work is done, she forgets it.
That is why it lasts forever.

Use the Magic Question early and often: ***What's important to you about that?***

Attract with the heart, or how to be irresistible

We talked about how to attract a man with your head: listen to him. We talked about how to attract a man with your body: radiate sensual energy. How do you attract with the heart?

A cross-cultural study I recall from some time ago concluded that kindness was the quality people valued most in a mate. There's no argument with that – compassion is indeed attractive. However, I think of the light of compassion as a diffuse one, like that of a lamp. As such, it may not be as effective at *attracting* a given guy. Have you ever heard a guy say, "Damn, that girl is so *compassionate* – I just can't stop thinking about her." Well, me neither.

However, your heart is the most powerful attractant you possess. And the way you turn that lamp of compassion into the laser of attraction is by practicing *devotion.*

Devotion is a potent force, and it is yours the moment you choose to embrace it. And as soon as you do, you become the Goddess. Because to express devotion completely, you must embody kindness, grace, sensuality, and all the other aspects of the divine feminine.

To express devotion, you need to set aside certain notions you may harbor from the past. The idea of *quid pro quo* does not work here – you must offer the devotion first (to a worthy recipient, we sincerely hope). You must quash any notion of 'what has he done for me lately.' You must set aside the ego completely, and allow yourself to become an instrument of divine love. Any energy spent holding up your own importance will nullify the practice. Devotion does not bicker; devotion does not demand; devotion does not possess. It is a flood of infinite giving and acceptance. It is like seed for the bird, the ocean for the fish: abundance, sustenance, the very gift of life.

If you are able to offer all of that and convey it through your face, body and voice, there is no man alive who can resist it. This is a great power which you possess, and with power comes responsibility. So you will wield this power only to the right kind of man, the worthy recipient, using your best judgment to find him.

In the meantime, you do have to *practice* conveying devotion so you get better at it. How else will you be prepared for Mr. Right when he arrives? Exactly. Ideally, you'd like to be able to get feedback from a male friend – preferably one who has no romantic interest in you whatsoever, since this is a powerful exercise (a gay friend would be ideal). Five minutes of honest feedback from a man can forever transform the way you present yourself.

Exercise 19. Practicing devotion.
Find a full-length mirror and stand in front of it. Get your digital camera if you have one. Now, as objectively as possible, rate your radiance on a scale of 1-10. How irresistible would a man find you right now? Where you start matters a lot less than where you end up, so just give yourself a number to get the ball rolling. Take the 'before' picture.

Now close your eyes and picture what it would look like if you were to convey complete and utter devotion to a man. How would you look into his eyes? What would your facial expression look like? At what angle would you bend your neck? How would you breathe? How would you move your body? How would you move?

As you start to do all of these things, open your eyes. Notice what it all looks like. Now, what can you do to make it even better? Make those adjustments. Take the 'after' picture.

Now give yourself a new number. How is it different from the first number you gave yourself? How long did it take to make that improvement? If you liked how this exercise affected you, resolve to do it every day when you're getting ready in the morning. Notice its effects over time.

Attract in the right order

If you were to bake a cake, would the order of how you did things matter? You'd probably end up with something interesting if you were to take some flour, put it in the oven at 425 degrees for 15 minutes, then take it out and splash some water and baking powder on it. But you'd have a different beast than if you were to follow the recipe step-by-step.

Likewise, there is a recipe when attracting a man. If the ingredients are head, heart and body, there is an order for presenting them that works well and others that work less well. As a member in good standing of the male species for over three decades and privy to men's personal thoughts on women for that long, I can tell you that there's a fairly set order, namely:

$$BODY \rightarrow MIND \rightarrow HEART$$

This will not come as a surprise to most of you. The man you will date will first find you physically attractive. Subsequently, if he finds compatibility on the mental plane as well, he will proceed to like you – a lot.

Sometimes men skip the middle part entirely and go straight to falling in love. This is more lust and infatuation than something more lasting, and there's nothing wrong with it – it has its time and place. Fun, perhaps, but solid three-chakra connection, less likely. Just be clear on what you're seeking.

Let's also discuss what this order is *not*. Mind almost never comes first, so if you're leading with that, don't necessarily expect a guy to fall for you. Heart also does not come first. If you're just kind and compassionate to a guy without sparking that physical attraction initially, you're putting the flour in the oven without making the dough first.

If it feels as if I'm mentioning the obvious, it's because I want you to avoid heartbreak and frustration down the line. If you're super-smart and witty and think, "Well, he should like me for my wit and brilliance – if he's just looking for a pretty face, I don't want him anyway," you're just wishing the world to be different than it is (i.e., creating pain for yourself). The Good Guy will appreciate your wit and brilliance for sure – *after* he has decided that he finds you pretty. There really is no way around that.

And you don't *want* there to be a way around that. Yes, there are exceptions, and they are rare, rare. That's why they're called exceptions. The solid three-chakra relationship will have as its basis a healthy sexual attraction, and if you don't have that at the outset, you're already starting on shaky ground. Be patient and wait for the guy who's the right fit instead of trying to shoehorn Mr. Wrong into the spot. Chances are you've done that at least once before (or know someone who did) and it didn't work, so take advantage of your own wisdom.

The physiology of attraction

There is a physiological basis for the different kinds of attraction we just touched upon. This is because fundamentally, feelings are created by neurotransmitters. In her book *Why We Love*, biological anthropologist Helen Fisher divides love feelings into three categories: lust, romance, and long-term attachment. Romance can trigger lust; lust can also trigger romance, but to a lesser extent. Attachment is a byproduct of lust and romance over the long term.

The hormone primarily responsible for lust is testosterone; adrenaline is also involved in mediating lust and short-term attraction. Romance (a.k.a. being in love) is mediated by dopamine and norepinephrine. Attachment is mediated by oxytocin in women and vasopressin in men.

The table below summarizes the various hormones and neurotransmitters involved in love feelings and how each one is evoked. Don't worry too much about which action evokes which substance; just know that all of the substances in the end increase attraction in some way.

Substance	**Evoked by...**	**Extra features**
dopamine	novelty	can increase testosterone levels
adrenaline	danger, excitement	thought to mediate love at first sight
norepinephrine	stimulants, novelty	
oxytocin (in women)	nipple & genital stimulation, orgasm, touch	creates long-term bonding
vasopressin (in men)	genital stimulation, touch, dehydration	
PEA	direct eye-gazing	mediates rapid attraction

Phenethylamine (PEA) is a particularly interesting chemical stimulated by looking directly into the eyes of another person. One study showed that looking directly into the eyes of a member of the opposite sex *for just two minutes* engendered passionate feelings in both people (Kellerman et al., 1989).

Without getting into too much scientific detail (for that I highly recommend Helen Fisher's books), just by looking at the table above we can reach some useful conclusions. Dopamine, adrenaline, norepinephrine, oxytocin and PEA mediate attraction-related feelings. So to evoke those feelings, you want to engage in *novel, exciting, physically- and emotionally-arousing activities,* and pepper those activities with *touch* and *direct eye-gazing.* You may look a little silly if you try to do those all at the same time; better just to know that these are the things that you should be doing, and sprinkle them in liberally till you do them regularly.

> **To evoke passionate feelings, gaze directly into his eyes and hold the gaze.**

Success and your integrity

These and other techniques may seem calculated, and to a certain extent they are. And you know what? There's nothing wrong with that. Evolution has offloaded a lot of the calculations in the mating game to your unconscious faculties, so calculations are happening all the time anyway. And all parties involved are doing what they can to improve their chances of success: makeup and clothing to enhance the appearance; fancy restaurants to create the ambience; cool cars to impress; sultry glances to entice.

So as much as we may dislike playing games, we have little choice in the matter. We're all doing it anyway. That's the Tao of it. So instead of struggling against the game, why not play to win! Most people do not play to win. Rather, they play to remain in their comfort zone while maintaining moral superiority. Play to win. As long as you do it with integrity and you're not intentionally hurting anyone (including yourself) in the process, it's the right thing to do.

To have these techniques work optimally, you have to find your own comfort level with them. If you know your intentions are good and there is a win for both parties, then by all means forge ahead. Also, ask yourself this: if being slightly more deliberate and disciplined than usual in dating means that both you and your date get to have a fabulous connection, a great time and a memorable experience, who loses here?

The idea is not to resort exclusively to manipulative tactics to get what you want, but rather to recognize the structure of human interactions and the effective steps required to achieve a certain outcome. This is merely the opposite of being sloppy and haphazard.

The Tao merely shows you the way the world works, without strict judgment about right or wrong. However, when you are aligned with your own inner feeling and integrity, you tend to become much more effective, and that is what I recommend. Enlightened self-interest is the way of the Tao.

The principle of *wu-wei*

We have gotten into several techniques in this chapter, so I want to emphasize something before we proceed any further. As a woman, you naturally possess all the techniques necessary to attract a good man. In other words, *you don't need any techniques.* This book merely serves to uncover your innate abilities, dust them off and bring them to the fore. When a technique harmonizes with your essential nature, it simply becomes a part of you. And kindness, open-heartedness, listening and devotion are not techniques – they are aspects of the divine you. Over time, they will not be something that you *do*, but rather *who you are.*

You will find that as you internalize the principles of the preceding chapters more and more and become the archetype of the divine goddess, you will worry less and less about what to do and find that things flow their own way. This is the way of the Tao:

> *In pursuit of knowledge,*
> *every day something is added.*
> *In the practice of the Tao,*
> *every day something is dropped.*

Less and less do you need to force things,
until finally you arrive at non-action.
When nothing is done,
nothing is left undone.

True mastery can be gained
by letting things go their own way.
It can't be gained by interfering.
            — Lao Tzu, Tao Te Ching, *Ch. 48*

The Taoists call this *wu-wei* — not-doing. Or more accurately, *wu wu-wei* — doing not-doing. And when you stop the doing, you will *be* someone — a woman who is the incarnation of the divine feminine.

Chapter 11. Romance, or what to do on a date

Stoking the fires

So you found a Good Guy. Congratulations. And you've managed to set up some time to spend together. This chapter is about specific things you can do to make those dates go exceptionally well, so you are in control of your destiny and in the best position to have a fulfilling interaction, however you define that for yourself. The prior chapter had the essential principles behind creating powerful, lasting attraction between you and the man – which, properly utilized, are more than enough. To ensure that you are as empowered as possible, I'd also like to share with you some specific techniques to empower you even further. This is beyond hair-flipping or lip-licking – that stuff you already know and don't need a guy to teach you. This is subtler business.

Rapport

One of my hypnosis teachers once said about personal interactions, "Inside of rapport, anything is possible; outside of rapport, nothing is possible." In sales, persuasion, relationships, or any kind of human transaction, rapport is *the* key to effective communication. If you learn nothing from this book except for how to establish and maintain rapport, you will be miles ahead of the rest of the pack.

As a woman, if you're practicing the preceding exercises – especially the one about listening – you will naturally be in deep rapport with a man and won't need to practice getting rapport. However, for the sake of completeness, I want you to have this powerful skill at your disposal.

I think of rapport as that familiar feeling of standing next to someone looking out at the rest of the world together, versus sitting facing one another, each with your own point of view. When you are in rapport, you become like the other person, and people tend to like people who are like themselves. Entire books have been written on this subject alone, but the essence of these can be conveyed in a small space. In this section, I will give you a triple treat: the traditional tools for rapport (which you should use regularly), the three secret techniques for rapport, and one counterintuitive method.

The key technique of nonverbal rapport is *mirroring*. If you watch two people in deep conversation, you may notice something eerie: their body postures tend to mirror one another. The image to keep in mind is that of the tête-àtête: two people hunched over at a table at the same angle, talking in conspiratorial tones. Basically, you are mimicking the body language of your interlocutor. You want to do this as closely as possible: he moves his hand, you move yours. He nods, you nod. Hardly anyone ever notices when he is being mirrored, because almost all body language is *unconscious*, which by definition is what we are not aware of at the conscious level.

Which movements of the body are more important? Where to start? The proper technique is to match from the macro to the micro. Start with general body posture, the position of limbs in space, and then move on to motion of hands, feet, fingers, neck angle and facial muscles. Once you've mastered that, you can start to mirror vocal tone, volume and tempo as well. And finally, for achieving ultra-deep rapport, you want to mirror diction by repeating *verbatim* what the person just said. This is not active listening – this is *word-for-word* repetition of what you just heard. I call this *backtracking*, and it's super effective.

One of the reasons why these techniques are so useful is that in order to do them right, you must pay complete attention to your companion. This in itself is enough to engender attraction.

Ideally, the nonverbal rapport protocol becomes a habit so ingrained that you use it unconsciously and all the time. In any case, you should still use the following three secret techniques for creating and enhancing rapport, especially in interactions with less time to establish pacing and leading:

1) *Assume rapport.* Imagine that the person you're speaking to is an old friend that you've known for at least three years. The attitude is more along the lines

of "Hey, good to see you again, buddy" than "How do you do, sir."

2) *Go into the emotional state of the bond.* What would it *feel* like if right now you were to bump into your long-lost friend that you haven't seen in three years? How thrilled would you be? How eager would you be to talk to her? Summon that same feeling and bring it to the interaction at hand.

3) *Share a secret.* Preface your statement with "Can I tell you a secret?," then go ahead and share. It need not be something earth-shattering or embarrassing; it need not even be about you: "I just really appreciate your style" works, as does "I just can't stand mosquitoes." The fact that you prefaced it as being a secret is enough.

To really grasp rapport, think of your best friend and how you interact with her. How do you greet each other? What sort of things do you talk about? How do you bring up a topic of conversation? Bring those qualities to the interaction to deepen rapport.

In deep rapport, you're not afraid of losing your audience – you've been friends for years, for example – and so you are more willing to antagonize each other, tease one another or be slightly rude. This brings us to the covert technique which I call the *rapport of anti-rapport.* If right from the outset of an interaction you start playfully teasing someone, the implication is that rapport is already so deep as to permit this. Paradoxically, this *creates* rapport.

Two caveats: first, it's important to do this *playfully* and not too seriously. Feisty (being contrary in a friendly way) is good; confrontational and hostile less good. Second, follow up the anti-rapport with the usual rapport techniques, using anti-rapport as the spice rather than the main course.

Every time you do something to deliberately break rapport without actually breaking it, you *strengthen* rapport.

How to create passion

Here's one of my favorite paradoxical tidbits of human dating behavior. The key to creating passion is the presence of *obstacles*. That which is gained with little effort is lost without much regret – easy come, easy go. Passion, on the other hand, is like water building up behind a dam: the more it builds up, the more urgently it wants to break through and express itself. It's pent-up energy aching for release. You don't get that kind of intensity, the rush of water rolling over things wild and uncontrolled, unless the dam had held it back first. So in order to create passion, you must do two things: *plant the seed*, then *create obstacles*, even if they don't initially exist.

Planting the seed means giving him something to think about. Ideally you want it to be something that runs in his head over and over again while you're not around. A story or well-placed compliment is good for that.

Then create obstacles. Play up the distance between you. Set up dates two weeks to a month in advance while building up anticipation for them in the interim. Or, if you feel particularly daring and dastardly, do all of the above – then postpone the date at the last minute for an extra day or two (*caution:* handle with care – more on this soon). Which would you prefer – a mediocre date tonight, or one next month that's guaranteed to go extremely well? Think of the great love stories of history. The idea of star-crossed lovers is as old as time, and it is precisely because of the seemingly insurmountable barriers between the lovers that the passion intensifies.

> ## To create passion, plant the seed of attraction, then create obstacles.

How to make a man fall in love with you

My friend Michelle is a beautiful, sophisticated and exceptionally intelligent woman of about 30 who lives in New York City. Because she's so damn smart, she doesn't find too many men who can go toe-to-toe with her. But every once in a while, a keeper comes along. That's when she gets all excited – and instantly loses her bearings and calls me asking what to do. I'll never forget the one time she asked me, point-blank, "Alex – how do you make a man fall in love with you?"

Never having had a man fall in love with me, I'm not qualified to answer that question. However, I have been a man for a while, and have fallen in love with women more than once. From those experiences and my forays into the scientific literature, I've come up with three ways that a man will fall in love with you.

1) The Natural Way. Consciously or not, every man has a mental archetype of the woman he desires, and once in a blue moon, he comes across that woman. If that woman happens to be you, and you also find him interesting, hallelujah – let the fireworks begin.

There isn't much you can really do to engineer this kind of love. A man is attracted to a certain body type, facial look, hair color, smell, cultural background, or any other number of random elements of which even he himself is not fully aware. You could resemble his first girlfriend from high school. You could be wearing that one perfume that drives him nuts (because his first girlfriend from high school used to wear it). Whatever it is, this is the love that cannot be planned. If it happens, great. If not, read on.

*2) **The Devious Dastardly Way.*** With enough determination, you can make any man fall in love with you, and the procedure is simpler than you think. It can be summarized in three words: *give, withdraw, repeat.*

Before I elaborate on this, I want to let you know that I consider emotional manipulation of any person to be just plain wrong. I have been on the receiving end of that kind of treatment, and it was no fun. So why am I including this manipulative method of making a man fall in love with you if I don't condone it?

I'm including it because I don't believe any woman would use this procedure *consciously*. However, through coincidence and circumstance, a woman could end up using this procedure *unconsciously*. And then she's got a man who's borderline stalking her, and she doesn't understand why. Now that you know how this works, it's more likely that you can prevent this inconvenience from happening.

Here's the essence of it. You start out by giving the man attention. You appear interested, give him your number, and maybe even set up a date. You are *giving*. And then – you cancel the date at the last minute. This is *withdrawing*, and it puts the man in a tizzy. He won't understand what happened, and will be hurt and confused. This is when you call him and apologize profusely (which is different from flaking, when you don't seem very invested at all). Some emergency came up, it could not be avoided, you're so sorry, can we reschedule? You're showing that you actually cared, but just couldn't show up. That's more of the giving.

Usually, he'll be so pleased that you're still interested that he'll accept your apology and agree to reschedule. Now you have the option of canceling again, or showing up and using the procedure *during* the date. You can be very flirtatious, giving him lots of compliments, touching him here and there, gazing lingeringly deep into his eyes. You may even give him a kiss on the cheek at some point, or make out with him. You are *giving*. But you cut the whole procedure short when he least expects it, and leave abruptly – something came up. You *withdraw*.

Once again, he will be frustrated and confused, thinking he was *so* close – what went wrong this time? He will think about you all the time and wait with bated breath for you to call him again. And with judicious timing, you enter his life again and give a little bit more, only to withdraw it later. Three rounds of give and withdraw should reduce any man to putty in your hands – if that is what you want. The man will be completely infatuated with you.

The key to making this work is this: when you are giving, give genuinely. You really are into him. It's just that something completely unexpected comes up everytime he's on the brink of being on solid ground with you. And that's when you withdraw completely, yanking the rug out from under him decisively and unequivocally – only to restore it later. In the case of my friend Brian, a woman broke up and got back together with him three times, each restoration of the relationship accompanied with vehement protestations of undying love (and passionate make-up sex). To this day, he can't recall being more obsessed with anyone, even though she was trouble.

By now, you see how deeply devious and manipulative this is. And by now, you may also realize that you may have unwittingly done something like this to some poor sap at some point in your life. You were initially interested, gave him your number, went out with him once or twice. But then you got busy – exams, big project at work – and he got relegated to the back of your mind. Then you thought about him again and responded to him positively, but then withdrew for some reason that wasn't entirely clear even to you. That's when he started acting clingy and weird, and you decided to ignore him – which, paradoxically, whetted his appetite even more, since you were withdrawing so completely.

So to keep from sending out the wrong signal to men, be more mindful of your actions towards them. On the other hand, if this is how you wish to nab Mr. Right, just know that you're playing with fire.

3) ***The High Road.*** If you are truly interested in a man and want him to grow in love, respect and admiration for you, this is the way to do it. The method is remarkably simple: bring out the best in him.

A man will steadily fall more and more in love with a woman who steadily helps him become more and more the man he has always wanted to be. As we discussed in Chapter 2, this is your opportunity to be the Goddess to his Warrior. Not only can you nurture the vision that he has of his own greatness, but you can go one step beyond and encourage him to be even bigger than he has imagined himself.

When you do this, he has no choice but to feel good about himself around you. He will feel taller, stronger, more capable, more masculine. And chances are that he's not getting anything like that anywhere else. Which means that he's more likely to stay with you for the long run.

Great idea, you say. But how do I do it?

How to bring out the best in a man

As conscious beings, we have the extraordinary ability to direct our energy according to our will. According to spiritual principle, energy goes where attention flows, so merely putting your attention on something will make it flourish. This is particularly true in our interactions with others.

Consider this scenario. Walk up to a stranger and say, "Why do you have to be such a jerk?" The most likely reaction you will get from him is, "Well, why don't you go to hell? You're the one who's being a jerk." By being nasty to someone, you will bring out and nurture the nastiness in him.

Contrast that with going up to someone and saying sweetly, "You look so nice today." The most likely response you'll get is something like, "Aww, that's so sweet of you! You look very nice yourself." By directing kind energy towards him, you brought out the kindness in him.

To put this in term of the language of devotion, address that energy of devotion to the part of the man you want to help grow. By consciously directing your energy, you can help another person along his (or her) path of evolution.

Every man you meet contains multitudes of archetypal characters within him – Boy, Warrior, Bully, Weakling, Prince, King, Rogue, Sinner, Saint, Magician, Trickster, Caveman. The way you interact with him and direct your energy at him has a large effect on the kind of man you end up dealing with. In essence, people rise to our expectations of them. Most of the time, this happens unconsciously. Here, I'm asking you to bring your unconscious expectations of men to conscious attention so you can direct your energy in a way to bring the greatest fulfillment to your life – and theirs, too.

The foolproof internal guide for your actions

There are so many ways to behave in response to men. How to know when you're doing the right thing? Should I call him back? How soon? Should I show more interest? Less? Instead of going through every possible scenario that can come up, I am now going to give you a foolproof tool for testing any action you could take to see whether or not it's the right way to go. It's called *running it through your own neurology.*

For example, let's say you're wondering whether you should send him a particular email. Send it to yourself first, read it a few hours later and see how it makes you feel. Generally, if you run a particular scenario through your own neurology and it feels in any way needy, boring, or desperate, it probably is. You're better off doing something else or nothing at all.

When you're unsure of what course of action to take, do an internal check by running it through your own neurology.

Incidentally, this is the basis of compassion: being able to put yourself in someone else's shoes. It's a useful skill.

What drives men away

For the past few years, I have been receiving stories about men and their dating experiences with women. Drawing upon that database and some of my own experiences, here are some behaviors that are highly effective in alienating a man. If you are interested in him in any way, even as just a friend, you want to avoid these behaviors at all cost.

There are at least three good reasons for avoiding these behaviors. First, if this was someone that you were interested in dating, then he's probably a worthwhile person to keep in your life even if things don't work out romantically. Also, you never know – somewhere down the road, you two may meet again under different circumstances, and you'll thank yourself for being on good terms with him.

That was the obvious reason. The second reason comes up particularly if you took my advice from earlier in the book and only dated men who were networked-in – that is, someone who was connected to your pre-existing social circle in some way.

Consider this: in the marketing world, studies have shown that a satisfied customer will on average tell two other people about his positive experience, while a dissatisfied customer will tell nine. Similarly, in the social marketplace, a man who's been treated poorly will tell his friends about it. So whenever you treat a man poorly, there are potential negative repercussions across your social network. The principle of enlightened self-interest then holds that, in the long term, you're better off treating everyone courteously.

The third reason is subtler. As we discussed earlier, psychologists have found that humans have an innate drive to avoid *cognitive dissonance*. This means that they have a strong desire to keep their thoughts consistent with their actions. So when we agree to do a small favor for someone, we back-justify and think, "Well, if I did that for him, it must mean I liked him." Similarly, if we do something nasty to someone, we tend to back-justify and think, "If I did that to him, it must mean that I *don't* like him." This can be a particularly pernicious feature of the human mind if you're not aware of it. For example, you could be *really* interested in a guy, but completely lose interest in him after you accidentally stand him up, even though he hasn't done anything wrong.

So if you want to get rid of a man for good, these are some excellent tactics. If you don't want to get rid of him, do yourself a favor and avoid these like avian flu. Here they are:

Canceling at the last minute, or 'flaking'. This is men's #1 pet peeve (according to a poll of 12,000 of my male readers). If you set up a date with a man and cancel without giving him enough time for him to reschedule – or even worse, if you stand him up – you've wasted his time and his good will. This is likely to jeopardize your chances with him, especially if he's a Good Guy. If he's *not* bothered by it, chances are that he either has little respect for himself or for you.

As Don Miguel Ruiz said in his *Four Agreements*, be impeccable with your word. The fabric of society is built on trust, and every time you break a promise, you weaken that fabric and shoot yourself in the foot. Extend to the men you date the same courtesy you would want them to extend to you.

How to recover from it: Unexpected things happen on occasion, thwarting even the best intentions – boss calls you in, family emergency comes up, you have a really bad coffee spill on your dress. So if you end up flaking on someone, take heart – recovery is fairly straightforward. Issue a sincere apology in as personal a manner as possible. A phone call is infinitely better than an email or text message. Then, offer *sincerely* (that word again) to make it up to him. Invite him to a show or a meal, or offer to cook dinner for him. Humility here is key. Then he can determine whether the make-up offer is sufficient.

The five emasculating behaviors. Whenever I conduct workshops for men, I do a values elicitation exercise. I ask a succession of questions to find out the thing that matters most to a man. Without exception so far, the highest value for a man ends up being *freedom.* Many spiritual teachers have commented on this, and one could say that complete freedom is the goal of the divine masculine.

Therefore it follows that anything that curtails this freedom emasculates the man, threatening to take him away from the divine masculine. Energy flows where attention goes, so when you give your attention to a certain aspect of a man, you are encouraging that part of him to grow, whether you like it or not. Some examples:

> 1) Overly solicitous attention: When you give a man this kind of attention, you are encouraging the *boy* in him to grow, denying his mature masculine. Unless that is your goal, reserve overwhelming solicitude for children under 12. Mothering is smothering.

> 2) Jealous attention: Questioning a man about his associations questions his warrior spirit and his devotion to you. Jealousy always has the effect of driving him away from you, which is the opposite of what's it's trying to accomplish.

> 3) Critical attention: Playfully teasing and challenging a man is great when done in moderation. Cutting him down is not.

> 4) Competing: Competition is a very masculine activity, so when you choose to compete with your man, you are risking destruction of the masculine-feminine polarity between you if you're not careful.

Now it has to be restored somehow. If he wins, you will feel put down; if you win, he will feel emasculated. Both those outcomes are terrible, so the safe path is to avoid competing with him entirely.

5) Correcting: Leave that for after you've started dating seriously. And even then, there are better and worse ways of doing it which are beyond the scope of this book (once again, I refer you to Gottman).

What to do about it: Emasculating behavior towards a man tends to be more of a habit than a one-time event. And since habits are unconscious, we tend not to be aware of them consciously. So the first step is to pay attention and notice if you're doing it. Listen to others (especially friends and other men) who say you're doing it. Then take steps to eliminate that behavior.

Neediness. Perhaps I should have mentioned this one first, because nothing will make a man run away faster. Men love it when you want them; they can't *stand* it when you act needy. It's the ultimate infringement on their freedom and they'll avoid it like the plague. Calling him too often, wanting to see him all the time, clinging to him like Saran wrap, worrying that he doesn't like you and he'll leave – these are the kinds of behavior that *will* make him leave. Fast.

What to do about it: Remind yourself that you are the complete, self-sufficient, loving goddess that you are. If you feel as if you're about to teeter into the needy zone, call a girlfriend or do something that changes your state, like taking a hike or going to yoga class. Afterwards, the feeling will be gone, and you'll realize it wasn't really you.

The five masculating gifts

There's a saving grace to the emasculating behaviors: if you do their opposite, a man will absolutely adore you. He will want to spend more and more time around you, since you are the source of these great feelings he's having. Even if you don't end up romantically involved with a man, doing these things will inspire a loyal friendship in him that's likely to last for years.

Don't let the length of this section belie its importance: these gifts are *priceless!* These are what a good woman does for a man. They are manifestations of love in action. These may also seem like the kind of things that you do once you're already in a relationship with a man, as opposed to when you're just dating. But if dating is the preview to the relationship and what determines whether it happens or not, why put anything but your best foot forward? There's no sense in saving yourself for later – the time to love is always right now.

Here are five suggestions for being the kind of woman who helps a guy grow into greatness.

Give him his freedom. Freedom is a man's most treasured possession. The more of it you give him, the more he will respect you and, paradoxically, the more he will want to run back to you. Even if you're crazy about a guy, resist the temptation to spend every waking moment with him. As one wise person said it, give him the gift of missing you. He'll just want to spend time with you that much more.

Give him your trust. The more you trust a man and allow him to take charge, the more he grows in the masculine. And if you're the agent of making him feel two feet taller than he normally does, he'll just seek out your company that much more.

Give him your bond. Heard of the expression "behind every great man is a great woman"? This is your chance to be that woman. When you consistently do as you say you will, a man will have deeper and deeper trust in you. This will make him feel as if he has a partner who really has his back. As a result, he will be bolder, bigger and stronger in everything that he does.

Give him your praise. It may not seem so, but we guys are actually kind of fragile inside. And it seems that a lot of scientists are convinced that everything we do is to impress women, from building large monuments to launching wars. In fact, evolutionary psychologist Geoffrey Miller makes a convincing case that we evolved such outsize brains mostly to enable skills that would impress mates.

So give the poor fellow some acknowledgment to make him feel as if the all the paintings he painted, the buildings he built, the poetry he scribbled and wealth he accumulated has been worthwhile. Praise him for the little things, for the attention he gives you, for his small victories. You will allow him to grow into the kind of man who is capable of even bigger victories – and of creating more monuments to you.

Give him your grace. Every boy slips every once in a while or does something naughty. We know you're smart, so we know that *you* know when we slip. As long as the slipping is not a regular occurrence, this is your opportunity to open your heart and offer the man redemption. A man will be eternally grateful for your giving him a second chance – and grow into a much bigger man as a result of your demonstration of faith.

The importance of closure

Ever gone on a date that went reasonably well and have a guy not call you afterwards? Or give your number to a man you found interesting, and not hear from him at all? Or worse, gather all your courage to give him a call, then not hear back? Sucks, doesn't it. Well then you shouldn't be doing that to guys either, because they feel the same way.

Just because of the way the numbers work, you're going to encounter a lot more men that you won't end up dating than those that you will. This means that you'll be turning down a lot of guys. I can't emphasize enough the importance to *do so graciously*. You don't need to explain yourself, but you do owe it to the guy to communicate clearly that you're moving on. Even a brief email or text message is infinitely better than blowing him off and not responding to him at all.

Men find women's lack of responsiveness psychologically distressing. Because when you don't respond, you're effectively saying that he's not even worth a measly little message saying 'go away'. It also puts them in a state of limbo, since they don't have any information to go on. Is she not interested, playing hard to get or just busy? About as fun as a poke in the eye.

There's a reason to give a man closure that goes beyond etiquette and respect, and that's enlightened self-interest. As we said before, if the man in question is networked-in, that means you'll have friends in common. Rudeness to him could reverberate through your social circle, damage your sterling reputation and make it more difficult to get dates with other good men. It also jeopardizes your potential friendship – why burn bridges?

Another bit of enlightened self-interest: if your goal is to signal lack of interest, your withdrawal of communication initially *whets* his appetite instead of dulling it. This is the opposite of what you're trying to accomplish, so just give the 'no thanks' to him straight. It's the courteous *and* smart thing to do.

That's all well and good, you say, but what do I actually tell him? What are the exact words? Here's a formula to follow:

1) Start with praise and appreciation. "Hey Jim, you're a great guy and I'm really glad we met."
2) State very clearly what's on your mind so there's no doubt. Again, lead with the positive: "We seem to get along (or: 'I enjoyed our time together' if it's after a date), but I don't think we're a great *romantic* match for each other."
3) Re-state your appreciation, and if you really would like to stay friends with him, give him the option to do so. If not, don't: "I'd value your friendship, so if you'd like to stay friends, I'd appreciate that. If not, I understand, and all the best to you." For extra bonus points, close with more praise: "I'm sure there's a girl out there who'd be very lucky to find a guy like you."

The effect that an artfully gentle turn-down like this has on a man is that he gets to feel good about himself and harbor no hard feelings – and *you* get to look like a superstar. Additionally, it's easier for you to communicate this information because now it's not as difficult a conversation as before.

> **When you decide to move on, always give the man the courtesy of closure.**

Some completely obvious guidelines for date etiquette

We hold these truths to be so self-evident that clearly none of you need to be told about them. The *really* obvious ones I'm not even going to elaborate on: Be punctual. Show up. Return his communication in a timely manner. Don't get sloppy drunk.

The following are worth mentioning because even though they're still obvious, they're useful to keep in mind. So for the sake of completeness, here they are:

Honor the interaction by turning your phone off. You've made plans to meet. You have cleared your schedule to make the meeting possible. So it only makes sense for both of you to honor the time and energy you have put into making the meeting happen. This means that you will do your best to minimize distractions and focus your attention on him.

Unless you have young children, chances are there's nothing requiring your immediate attention while you're out on a date. And if you do expect odd phone calls, do your best to minimize them beforehand. Every time you pick up the phone during a date with a man, you are essentially saying that this other thing is more important than he is. If that's what you intend to convey, no problem. If not, keep the phone off.

Here's a story that illustrates that. Dan was on a first date with a lovely young lady named Brigitte. It was a beautiful summer evening in Boston's Botanical Gardens, and they were getting along very well. One moment, as they were holding hands, their eyes locked, and they drew closer together, face to face. Right then Brigitte's phone rang. For a moment, they both froze, as Dan said to himself, "Please please *please* don't answer it." That's when Brigitte reached into her handbag, whipped out the phone, looked at the caller

234

ID and said, "It's my mom," and proceeded to talk to her for a few minutes. Dan waited for Brigitte's conversation to conclude, said, "I have to go now," and left right then and there. He never called Brigitte again. As Dan put it, "There is no bigger buzzkill than going for that first kiss with a woman – and her mom calls and she picks it up." Don't pull a Brigitte.

Stay focused on your companion. There will always be distractions in the environment where you meet with a man. Do your best to stay focused on your date in spite of those distractions. Not only is a wandering attention inconsiderate, but it also disrupts the rhythm and flow of a date, especially if the date's going well. A good rule of thumb is that something that keeps you from interacting with your date for more than 10 minutes is best avoided entirely. Some examples of these distractions: shops; TV screens; other people, especially friends you bump into or other men you could appear to be flirting with; uncomfortable footwear; and visiting the ladies' room.

Let him speak uninterrupted. When your date is speaking, let him speak. Once he's done, he will stop and signal that it's your turn. While he's talking, resist the temptation to chime in with your helpful comments, witticisms, or even empathy ("Oh my god, that happened to me last week, too"). If he's started a story, let him finish it, no matter how long-winded it seems – especially if *you* asked him to tell the story.

Allow yourself to be led. I wrote this book specifically with career women in mind. So you are probably used to directing things, managing things, fixing things and generally getting stuff done. You have mastered some principles of masculine energy, and more power to you for that. What I'm asking you to do is to tone down that masculine energy when you're on a date and allow your feminine energies to flourish some.

There are many good reasons for this. First, as we touched on before, a man is most likely interested in you not because of how good a man facsimile you are but rather because you are a woman, the very source of feminine energy and the complement to his masculine energy.

Second, it allows you to assess accurately the man's suitability as a potential partner. This is your chance to let go and allow someone to take care of you for a change, so embrace that opportunity. And it's his chance to showcase for his ability to take care of you. The more you allow him to take over and put on his show, the more useful data you are getting on him. Does he open the car door for you? Does he take your hand as you were crossing the street? Does he offer to pay for dinner? Does he offer his arm as you were walking in the park?

These may seem like small things, but they tend to be accurate indicators of a man's trustworthiness and leadership ability. If he doesn't do these things, he may not be the right man for you. And if you walk in front of him when crossing a street or offer to pay your share of dinner, you are denying yourself this very useful information.

Now both you and I know that you're perfectly capable of crossing a street on your own and paying your own way. That is not the point. The point is that human courtship is a dance. And as in ballroom dancing, it's the man's job to lead. The point of dancing is not to get anywhere – it is to dance together. And for the partnership to have a chance of success, you must allow yourself to be led. If you feel that you could do a better job of leading the dance, you may be with the wrong partner. It's also possible that you need to relax, let go of the reins, and just for a moment, surrender to the idea of letting him lead. Just see where it takes you. It could be a lot of fun.

Getting physical and the art of tantalizing

Let's be frank: a big reason why you bother dating at all is to find someone you can get intimate with physically. Touching, massage, cuddling, rolling around naked with someone and having sex are all great fun.

Now because of your privileged position as the woman, you are usually the gatekeeper and pacesetter when it comes to physical intimacy. And it doesn't take much to get a guy physically intimate with you: a hair flip accompanied by a smile usually suffices.

As we described, most men are ready to capitalize on a sexual opportunity when it presents itself, so there's not a lot of art involved in getting a man to kiss you, or even to get him in bed. All you have to do is ask. The art is getting what *you* want, *with whom* you want, on *your* terms.

So first we need to figure out what you're on the market for: a roll in the hay, a fling, or a boyfriend. Then adjust the method depending on your desired outcome.

The method is blissfully simple, and you know it already. It's called *teasing*. This means giving the man a little of what he wants, then withdrawing. It's the physical manifestation of one overarching idea which could be the subtitle for this book: *always leave him wanting more*. This is so important that I'm going to say it again: always leave him wanting more. And I'm going to put it in a box like this:

Always leave him wanting more.

I believe I've made myself clear here. Of course, men are going to string me up by the privates for telling you this, but it's true: men secretly love to be teased (or tantalized, to use a word with a more positive connotation). Yes, sometimes we get exasperated with it, but deep down inside, we wouldn't want it any other way. Especially a smart, well-to-do Good Guy will welcome the challenge of dealing with a woman who has the self-control and savvy to be a master tantalizer.

Now I can just hear some of you saying, "No! I refuse to play such silly games. I'm not going to torment men, especially the ones I like." Well, alright, fine. However, as we discussed already, if you're dating, you're playing a game whether you like it or not. There are rules – albeit fuzzy, unwritten ones – moving towards an outcome, so you're already involved in a game by definition. I just want you to play it well so you enjoy the process and get something positive out of it. And nobody's asking you to torture anyone. We're just asking you to demonstrate a little bit of self-discipline.

As much as I wish I didn't have to recommend this course of action, it's just so much better than the alternative. Tantalizing is the opposite of giving a man all you've got all at once on the first request. That's just giving away the store and relinquishing all your power and leverage in the dating process. It's the difference between burning up the fuel in your car's tank little by little, versus setting the whole thing on fire at once. The former method is likely to get you more mileage.

Again, moderation is key, since it's easy to overdo the tantalizing. You withdraw the favor from the man just long enough to *whet* his appetite, not obliterate it. Tantalizing is an implicit promise of future fulfillment, so if you delay the fulfillment too much or don't intend to deliver any at all, you may end up being resented as a Tease (bad thing) versus celebrated as a Tantalizer (good thing). Once again, the middle path of the Tao is best. Do it without overdoing it.

There are scientific reasons why this works. When you give a man a little bit of what he wants, you're creating a positive stimulus. This gives him a little dose of feel-good neurotransmitters. While he awaits the next stimulus, he's building *response potential* – basically, a damming-up of neurotransmitters waiting to release. Anticipation creates response potential, but only up to a point, after which it decays back to normal (often causing resentment in the process). So you don't want to delay too much, remembering that *gratification*, not delay, is still the key ingredient in delayed gratification.

Now, when you deliver the next timely stimulus, he gets a *bigger* jolt of neurotransmitters than he did the first time. So you're really doing him a favor by tantalizing him, since he gets to have *more* fun than he would have otherwise had. Moreover, when you give too much positive stimulus too soon, you risk blunting his response (through a phenomenon called *habituation*), which we'll discuss more in the next chapter. Do you feel better about the whole tantalizing thing now?

When it comes to getting physical, the man will usually take the lead, so you tantalize by granting or denying permission to his advances. Feel free to take the physical lead on occasion yourself. The rule is simple: you may only take a step forward after you've taken one step back. Depending on how fast you want things to progress, you can go two steps forward, one step back; three steps forward, one step back; four forward, three back – whatever suits your fancy. Test it out for yourself and find out what works best for you.

As a woman, I have no doubt that you're already a master at this. But *just* in case this all sounds too abstract, here are some simple examples to clarify the whole step-forward, step-back protocol:

• Massage his arm, then his shoulders; then go back to the arm before getting to the neck.

• Kiss him on the neck, then on the cheek, then go back to the neck before getting anywhere close to his lips.

• Touch him on the chest, then the belly, then go back to the chest before venturing any further south.

So you want a second date

A frequent question I get from my female readers is "How do I get the second date?" My answer: wrong question! You, the pursued party as decreed by nature, the embodiment of the divine feminine, the wellspring of infinite compassion, source of more devotion than he's ever received, should never have to worry about that. And if you've been putting into practice what we've discussed so far, *he* will be the one begging to see you again. Your job is to draw him out and evaluate whether he's a Good Guy – and a potential match for you. You are the evaluator. You are the picky buyer. You are in the driver's seat.

That said, I still want to make sure that you get the second date, so *leave him wanting more* (ah, that again). Remember the legend of Scheherazade in the *1001 Arabian Nights*? She would tell a story to the bloodthirsty King Shahryar each night and cut it off right at the cliffhanger, leaving the king in such a state of suspense that he had to grant her a day's reprieve from execution to hear the rest of the story the next day. For you it's not your life on the line, but it is something fairly important: your fulfillment. So play your hand well and be the cliffhanger.

Whenever I give you an idea, I also like to give concrete examples of how to use it, so here are some suggestions:

Leave open conversational loops. Wow, I just thought of something incredibly important to tell you, but I'll have to share it with you later.

What did I just do? I opened a conversation topic – without quite finishing it. That's an open loop. The unconscious mind of your listener will crave closure and want to hear the rest. For example, you'd say, "That reminds me of a trip I took with my sister to Carnaval in Brazil – it was *sooo* much fun... but we can get back to that later." Missing information is mystery, and mystery increases your attractiveness. So open some loops with the promise of closing them later – and your King Shahryar (minus bloodthirsty intent) will want to come back for more.

Leave open physical loops. If you give good hand massages and you massage both his hands, you close the loop. If you just massage one hand, he will wonder when the next hand gets the attention, and you'll have an open loop. If you kiss him good-night on the cheek but not on the lips, you're creating an open loop. Next time, if you kiss him on the lips but keep your mouth closed, you're creating another open loop. You get the idea: leave him wanting more.

You're overdoing it when you're sabotaging your own fun purely for the sake of form. If you're dying for a torrid makeout session with the man of your dreams and you know you're not going to see him until you come back from your monthlong business trip, by all means go for it. You can be savvy without turning into a nun.

Hint at future shared activities. When you find out things you have in common, describe what it would be like to do it together: "Oh my god, we should definitely go do a salsa class together! I really enjoy dancing, and love it when a man leads well on the dance floor." Now he's imagined himself having a good time dancing with you, holding you in his arms and twirling you around, and if it doesn't happen, it's a *perceived loss* for him. People are much more motivated to prevent loss than they are to go for gain, so he's now more likely to want to see you again.

Give him a chance to shine. Did he say he could beat you at air hockey? That he makes a mean lasagna? Bring it on, you say – on the next date. You're giving him a chance to show you how cool he is (guys love that) *and* ensuring yourself a subsequent meeting, you crafty woman.

What you don't want to do too often is to issue the man a challenge. That's one of the emasculating behaviors we just covered. Challenging a function of the *masculine* – the kind of thing his guy buddies are for. If you challenge him, you risk compromising the yin-yang polarity. In the meantime, you *are* craftily setting up an opportunity to make him look good. When he looks good, he feels good, he attributes that good feeling to you, and he will want to see you again. And even if you're the world air-hockey champion, when you let him win (by the smallest of margins, of course), you both win in the long term.

Physical intimacy: timing it right

The question "How do I know it's the right time to sleep with a guy?" has been and always will be a perennial favorite. True, as the woman, you may have most of the sexual power in the relationship. If you want sex to happen, it usually does, and if you don't want it to happen, it doesn't. However, this does not make your predicament any simpler. If you move too fast, does that reflect on your character and reputation? If you take too long, will his ardor cool? Should you initiate? Is there such a thing as having too much experience? Or not enough? What will he think?

What I really like about the Taoist way of thinking is its simplicity. Now the *Tao Te Ching* does not address the question of sex directly. However, there is the passage from Chapter 23 which I find relevant to this topic:

> *Express yourself completely,*
> *Then keep quiet.*
> *Be like the forces of nature:*
> *When it blows, there is only wind;*
> *When it rains, there is only rain;*
> *When the clouds pass, the sun shines through.*
>
> *If you open yourself to the Tao,*
> *You are at one with the Tao*
> *And you can embody it completely.*
> *If you open yourself to insight,*
> *You are at one with insight*
> *And you can use it completely.*
> *If you open yourself to loss,*
> *You are at one with loss*
> *And you can accept it completely.*
>
> *Open yourself to the Tao,*
> *Then trust your natural responses;*
> *And everything will fall into place.*

So I would imagine that if the *Tao Te Ching* were to answer the 'when' question we posed at the beginning of this section, the answer would be simple, succinct, and come mostly from within you. It may even sound like this: *you should only have sex when you really want to.*

Assuming that you're clear with your own motivations and that you've done your homework and picked a Good Guy, that guideline should suffice. It may sound simplistic, but consider this. There are people out there having sex when they *don't* want to. And there are plenty of people *not* having sex when they really want to. Those policies aren't necessarily aligned with your fulfillment.

Notice also that the 'when you really want to' policy exists in the *now*. We're all for foresight, but you simply don't have access to the future – all we have is the present. Also, dwelling on the past and the way things unfolded the last time and the time before isn't going to be helpful either. It's you, your guy, your desire, and your best judgment *right now*. So quit overthinking it already.

It's also free of any notions of guilt, shame, and opinions of third parties. The ancient Taoist masters thought of sex as sacred communion between two consenting adults. Practiced properly, it is a path to improved health, longevity, and spiritual development. This simple, straightforward formulation, plus the absence of the concept of sin in Taoist thought, is in contrast to the complications that certain religious traditions heap upon sexual intimacy.

Whatever religion you were raised in and however old you are today, it's never too soon to relinquish all those extra complications that get in the way of your fulfillment. Let's face it: sex is fun, and you enjoy it. A lot. And there's absolutely nothing wrong with that. In fact, it means you're a healthy, vivacious woman with the forces of nature coursing freely through your veins. Amen to that.

At the same time, sexual energy is a powerful force. To ensure that it's a source of fulfillment in your life, it's important to use it judiciously. It's a bit like a tiger: let loose untamed, it can cause damage; tamed, it can serve you. That's why we're saying *when you really want to* as opposed to *whenever you want to*. That's the difference between the tiger tamed and the tiger let loose, a constructive force and a potentially destructive one.

So let go of all the arbitrary labels. Sex isn't right or wrong or dirty or clean – it simply is. You're not a slut if you've slept with several men (whatever several means to you). And you're not a prude if you take your time to get physically intimate with someone. You're just you. Suspend judgment, and see things simply as they are.

Balancing desire and empowerment

It's no news to you that sex is a major motivator of men in their pursuit of women. So if you were to offer it up too early, you stand to lose some leverage in the relationship. However, if you're really good at sex, you will probably *gain* leverage once you start sleeping together, since he'll be coming back for more. So the more skilled you are sexually, the earlier you can afford to initiate sexual relations with a man without losing leverage.

I've mentioned the word *leverage* a few times here, so let me make something clear: sex is, above all, a shared experience of joy, not a business transaction. The joy is tarnished when it's used as a bargaining chip or a tool to manipulate and control. At the same time, I do want you to be aware of how initiating sexual activity relates to your empowerment and long-term fulfillment in a relationship. Awareness is good.

If there's a downside to jumping into things too early, there's also a downside to delaying too much – namely, loss of your own fulfillment. Allow me to illustrate with an example. Let's say you bought yourself a nice slice of chocolate cake, and you're saving it for a time to really enjoy it. You think about it at work, imagining how delightful it would be to go home and, after a long day of work, treat yourself to this luscious dessert.

You get home, open the refrigerator door, look at the slice of cake, and think, "Well, if I have it *tomorrow*, it'll be even better, because I'll want it that much more." So you wait another day. And perhaps another day. On the third day, when you finally take out the chocolate cake, you notice a little white spot on it – it's started to spoil, and it's no longer good to eat. You ruefully throw the cake in the trash, and with it, the promise of fulfillment. The middle path of the Tao here is balancing your own fulfillment with your leverage in the relationship so you get to eat your cake while remaining empowered.

Also keep in mind that you gain some very valuable pieces of information after having sex with a man. First is whether he's really after you or just wants sex. If the former, then he'll usually be more interested after sleeping with you. If he was just looking for another notch on his bedpost, his interest will wane.

Second, you get to find out if you're sexually compatible with each other. It's best to find that out sooner rather than later. A prolonged and intense non-physical romance can lead to a lot of frustration if you find out late in the game that you're really not right for each other sexually, which is the topic of the next section.

The importance of sexual compatibility

We discussed this briefly in Chapter 10 on the three-chakra connection, and it is important enough to bear repetition. If you aim to have a long-term relationship with a man, it's paramount that you be sexually compatible to one another. This is the story of the impending divorce or breakup I've heard a thousand times: "Oh, he's so great on paper, and we have everything in common, and he's just the sweetest guy, and I know I *should* be hot for him, but there's just no sexual chemistry."

There is no such thing as *should* be hot for him, sister – you either are or you're not. And it's called chemistry because it has everything to do with chemicals in your body and your genetic design. Without getting too much into the science here, there are deep-seated reasons why nature determines whether two people are sexually compatible that bear upon the health of their potential offspring. For example, nature has built-in systems for making siblings sexually unattractive to each other, since their kids could potentially come out with three heads and five limbs.

This is the Tao operating at its most basic, so heed its call. If you're sexually incompatible with a guy, there's probably a very good reason for it. So no matter how wonderful he is otherwise, it's a non-starter. Find your long-term mate elsewhere.

Men's secret fears about sex

Here's a little secret for you: men feel just as much confusion, guilt and shame around sex as you do. Most men you meet probably grew up under some religious tradition with myriad restrictions and prohibitions on sexual behavior. On some level, they probably think sex is dirty. Moreover, the decent, smart, educated guys you'll be dealing with are often afraid of being sexually aggressive. Between their sensitivity, respect for women, and fear of being accused of sexual harassment (or worse), they're scared little puppies deep down inside.

What an extraordinary opportunity for you! Because if you choose to be the one woman who can make sex feel like a guilt-free, shame-free, fun, liberating, shared experience for him, he will love you *forever*. There's the old cliché about men wanting a woman who's both the Madonna and the whore. You can toss that one out the window and replace it with what men really want (but may not know it yet): the goddess of love, all-nurturing, all-embracing, all beautiful all the time (refer back to Chapter 2, 'Who You Really Are').

Guys are scared. Yet at the same time they're supposed to be in charge of moving things forward, so it's really important for you to give them green lights so they know when it's okay to proceed. Otherwise, he may just get stuck between his two competing imperatives of 'stop' and 'go'. Verbal and non-verbal feedback are great, so if you're enjoying yourself and you want more – let him know! Make the green lights clear and unmistakable in their meaning, e.g. "Touch me there"; "More, please"; touching him; taking his hand or head and putting it where you want it to be. In fact, this is important enough to deserve its own box:

Clearly communicate to him when it's okay to proceed physically.

Remember again that if you've set things up the right way so far, this is the area you have to worry about the least. When you feel connected with a man and it feels right, it will flow. At that point, you will not need any rule book; trust yourself and flow with the Tao.

The importance of sexual know-how

One of the absolute best, most useful and productive things you can do in this lifetime is to educate yourself about sexuality. As a woman, you're basically designed to be a pleasure machine, so the better you get to know the machine, the more fun you'll have. It's free, it's safe, it's healthy, and it empowers you tons.

On top of that, sex is a pathway to higher consciousness and ecstatic communion. The Eastern sages have worked for millennia to figure out how to get the most out of it. Sadly, in spite of the abundance of information available on sexuality, most people remain undereducated on the subject. That is why we'll soon offer the booklet *The Tao of Sexual Ecstasy* as an introduction to Eastern and Western practices for enriching your sex life. So now, not only do you have my full permission to get really good at this, you no longer have an excuse not to.

There's a difference between skill and experience. To use an analogy, you can play tennis with a lot of people, but unless you get some proper instruction, there's no guarantee that you'll be any good. On the other hand, you can gain a lot of skill from a little bit of instruction, putting you head and shoulders above others who may have had more partners. So don't feel as if you need to sleep with a bunch of men to gain sexual skill. And if you've already slept with a bunch of men, don't feel as if that means you can't stand to learn more. Be open to the idea of real development in this area of your life. Anything worth doing is worth doing exceptionally well, especially when it's this much fun.

Have you downloaded your digital bonuses yet? Well, if you haven't, you should. You can get them here:

www.taoofdating.com/goddess

Part IV
Have

Chapter 12. Have: Making Relationships Last

How to keep a man worth keeping

"How do I keep him?" is the second most common question I receive from women readers (after "How do I get him?"). Well, that's a question about maintaining a relationship once it's established, and this book is more about dating. Still, I'd like to share with you some brief suggestions on making relationships last, and then refer you to the experts in that domain, especially the excellent work of Professor John Gottman.

The good news is that the way of the Tao is the way of effortless flow, the path of least resistance. So by continuing to do what you've been doing so far, you've gone a long way towards setting up a lasting relationship without further tweaks. Physics talks about the importance of initial conditions: the way a reaction is set up determines what course it's going to take over time. If you think of dating as one big reaction, then how you set things up determines how the rest unfolds.

And you've done a lot so far. You've instilled the right beliefs in yourself so you're coming from a place of self-sufficiency, abundance and goddess-consciousness. You've been practicing the right attitudes to give you the best results. You're clear on what kind of relationship you want. You've been going to the venues where you can find the right kind of man – the Good Guy with whom you can have a three-chakra connection. You use your body language strategically to get the interaction started. On a date, you project attentiveness and devotion and are a master listener. You make him feel 10 feet tall and inspire him to greatness. Your teasing skills drive him wild while keeping you empowered. And, in the end of it all, you're phenomenal in the sack. Now exactly what kind of fool would want to leave you?

That paragraph above pretty much summarized the entire book, and it represents a fair amount of work. But once you do it, you're in the *wu-wei* zone. There's no more deliberate doing, struggle or striving involved. You *are* where you want to be. And where you are is *always* a journey – there is no destination in life, ever. You are constantly moving, unfolding, growing – remember *anatta* or no-self. So the way to *keep* the guy (the 'destination') is the same as the way to *get* the guy (the 'journey'): Listen. Pay attention. Connect on the three chakras. Make him feel great about himself. Treat him exceptionally well, while leaving him wanting more (stay tuned for the upcoming *How not to be taken for granted* section).

Connect at three chakras for a lasting relationship

I'd like to elaborate a little on this topic that we introduced in Chapter 10. If you want to have a relationship that brings you lasting fulfillment, find a man with whom you can have that three-chakra connection of mind, heart and body. A couple that grows together stays together, so you want to be able to grow at all three levels with your man.

To emphasize the importance of having a strong connection at all three levels, let's do a little thought experiment to see what happens when you're with a guy with whom you connect on only two levels:

• Head and heart: The conversation's great, you absolutely respect the guy and love him deeply – *like a brother*. Sexual chemistry's weak, and you find yourself perpetually distracted by men out there who fire your loins in a way that Mr. H&H simply can't. You feel as if you need to be the aggressor to get anything started, getting too much into your masculine. You are frustrated and unfulfilled.

• Head and body: The conversation's great, and you're physically all fired up for each other, so the sex is great, too. But this is just not the guy who can own your heart, and you crave that deep connection of spirit which you suspect he may never be able to share with you. Without that, you feel as if you can't fully give of yourself or allow your divine feminine to flourish in receptivity and nurturance. You are frustrated and unfulfilled.

• Heart and body: You love this guy, and the sex is great. But he's kind of slow to catch on and can't really hold up his end of the conversation. He feels intimidated by your intellect and thus never can stimulate you in that department. Since you're one wicked smart cookie, you are frustrated and unfulfilled.

I went through that whole academic exercise to drive home a point: *do not settle*. If you're after a long-term relationship, go for the guy with whom you connect on all three levels.

Another very important point: get rid of the notion that you will ever *train* a man into the image of what you want him to be. That goes against the Tao – you're wishing the world to be different than it is and trying to shoehorn it into how it *should* be, which is the original formula for pain. As amazing and wise as you are, and as transformative the power of your love, teaching turtles to fly remains a losing proposition. Believe me, the guy who's already where you want him to be is out there waiting for someone exactly like you, so do both of you a favor and find *him* instead.

> **Select the man who's already where you want him to be instead of trying to train one who may never get there.**

Depth in a relationship vs. direction

One of my teachers said that the feminine principle in a relationship is its depth, and the masculine principle is its direction. As such, you the woman are in charge of deepening the relationship, while the man determines *where* it's going. This reflects in society at large where men ask the women to marry them, not the other way around. So pay attention if you find yourself taking over the direction of the relationship, since that's the *masculine* function.

Asking for commitment prematurely would be an example of such a thing. One of my favorite chapters of the *Tao Te Ching* is number 36:

> *If you want to shrink something,*
> *You must first allow it to expand.*

256

If you want to get rid of something,
You must first allow it to flourish.
If you want to take something,
You must first allow it to be given.
This is called the subtle perception
Of the way things are.

The soft overcomes the hard.
The slow overcomes the fast.
Let your workings remain a mystery.
Just show people the results.

You can't *take* commitment, but you can allow it to be offered. You do that by being the woman that any man would be silly not to commit to (and if he doesn't – don't you have better things to do with your time than hanging out with silly men?).

Of course it's less about whether or not the guy is silly than whether or not there's a fit between the two of you. If you are deepening the bond between you and there is a good fit, the rest should flow without further *doing* and effort – remember *wu-wei*, not-doing. And if you're not getting the fulfillment you want out of the relationship, it's probably not a good fit, and you can (and should) move on.

Leave the cage door open

The Eastern sages remind us that all things are temporary, and relationships are no exception. Even the best ones end in death or divorce. So keep a light grip on things. Think of a relationship as a handful of sand: if you hold it with upturned, relaxed hands, you get to keep it. If you squeeze the handful, you'll lose it all.

Squeezing the sand is a metaphor for attachment. The more tightly you try to hold on to something, the more likely you are to lose it. If there were a concept of sin in Taoist thought, attachment would be the biggie. So go ahead and love without attempting to possess.

Loving someone means wanting the best for him, and sometimes that means letting him go. That's why it's important to leave the cage door open, otherwise you'll never know when someone's sticking around under duress or of his own volition. It doesn't make a lot of sense to insist on keeping someone around who doesn't really want to stay. So let a man know that he has his freedom. It's the only way to keep him sticking around.

How not to be taken for granted

One of the main factors contributing to the demise of long-term relationships is being taken for granted. All those things that made you wonderful, interesting and special when you two first met are now simply accepted as standard features. It can even reach a point sometimes where just a small lapse from wonderfulness is held against you. Unfair, right?

Well, actually, this is completely normal and expected. There's nothing sinister about it. In fact, it's a demonstration of *habituation*, one of the main features of all nervous systems and a cornerstone of adaptability. As computer scientists would say, it's not a bug, it's a feature, and it's not going away. So learn how to work with it, not against it. Be like water, as the Taoists say. The obstacle's there, so instead of trying to topple it, figure out a way to go around it instead.

To optimize survival, the nervous system has evolved to notice change and filter out the background. It happens in all of your five senses: eyes notice moving objects and not static ones; you stop noticing the refrigerator's hum after a few days; you stop smelling something after five minutes. This is called *habituation*, and there are mechanisms operating at the *cellular* level to make this work. In other words, you're better off understanding it and working *with* it rather than struggling against it (the Tao again). And the proper way to circumvent habituation is to deliberately introduce salient, unpredictable stimulus, better known as *change*. In other words, be a little unpredictable.

There are infinite ways of being unpredictable, but here I want to give you two techniques derived from behavioral psychology and animal training.

The first is deliberate unpredictability, especially when it comes to doing nice things for your partner. Behavioral psychologists and animal trainers call this implementing an *irregular schedule of reinforcement.* Let's say you've been training a dolphin to jump, and you've been rewarding it with a single fish each time. The fish is the *reinforcer* – something that increases the chances of the behavior happening in the future. Now if you keep up the one fish-one jump regimen, after a while the dolphin will stop jumping as high. This is not because the dolphin is temperamental or evil – it's just the way things work neurologically.

The way to make sure that the dolphin's response doesn't decay over time is, paradoxically, to withhold the fish for a while. Give it to the dolphin every third or fifth jump. If you withdraw it entirely, the reinforced behavior will stop, so keep up the reinforcer; just give it *irregularly.* Now a funny thing happens: the dolphin starts to jump *higher* in order to get its reward. On some level, it has realized that just showing up isn't enough; it has to work harder.

If you think you're a lot smarter than a dolphin, let me ask you this: Has your interest in a man ever increased after he's said he's not interested? Have you ever started calling a man even more *after* he stops returning your calls in a timely fashion? The fact is, people *are* a lot smarter than dolphins, which is why this technique works even *better* for them.

To get you started, think of some behaviors involving reinforcement. We are unconsciously using reinforcers all the time in our relationships: praise, enthusiasm, food, presents, backrubs, sex. Anything that makes someone feel good is potentially a positive reinforcer. Become aware of them. Now think of all the ways that you use those reinforcers in a *habitual* manner, i.e. without thought or variation. Take kissing, for example. Do you kiss him every time you leave for work? Do you kiss him every time you come back? Do you kiss him in the same way, for the same duration? If you do, your kiss no longer conveys any information – it has become meaningless. Stop it already.

For example, make the standard back-from-work kiss the exception rather than the rule. Then change the way you do it. Kissing is just one example. You have probably fallen into habit in the way you go out with him, have sex, buy him presents, or sound happy on the phone. These are all opportunities for introducing variability.

Maybe the last two paragraphs got you down a little bit. You're thinking, "Look, I have a good heart, and I just enjoy doing nice things for my baby." That's great! As long as your enjoyment is the *main reason* you're doing it (vs. force of habit or even worse, trying to please), you will be naturally unpredictable and will never be taken for granted. This is an extension of the principle of enlightened self-interest. And as long as you're not doing the same thing over and over again, that's a fine policy.

For all the sweet women out there who really, really want to do nice things for their companions, here's another technique that works. This is called the *jackpot*. A jackpot is a larger-than-usual reinforcer, usually given for no reason at all. For the dolphin, it would be a big ol' mackerel instead of the little minnow it was usually getting. Human beings call it a *surprise*. For it to work, the jackpot has to be a reinforcer (i.e. pleasant), bigger than average, and unexpected. A full-body massage or tickets to the game work well; an offer to wax his chest or two tickets to your favorite ballet work less well.

It's worth repeating that the jackpot works because it's *unexpected*. Twice a year may be all you need for it to be maximally effective. Human beings (especially men) catch on very, very quickly, and if you do a jackpot every month, he'll come to *expect* his monthly surprise, in which case it's no longer a surprise. So take the middle path and do it without overdoing it. For an in-depth understanding of behavioral techniques, I recommend Karen Pryor's *Don't Shoot the Dog*. It's a fascinating read in its own right and tremendously insightful about human nature.

The four horsemen: recognizing communication problems before they arise

John Gottman, Professor of Psychology at Washington University, has been studying married couples for 25 years and has come up with a lot of interesting, highly accurate ways of evaluating the health of a relationship. In fact, using a 3-minute video of a couple interacting with each other, he predicts the success or failure of a marriage with over 90% accuracy. Although he studied married couples, his findings are instructive for long-term relationships in general.

What he has found is that there are certain styles of interaction that tend to be harbingers of doom for a relationship. The worst four amongst these he calls 'the four horsemen', since they tend to be, well, apocalyptic in their destructiveness. They are *criticism, contempt, defensiveness* and *stonewalling*. If you fall into these communication styles on occasion, that's okay – everybody does to some extent. The problem arises not when they happen every once in a while, but when they become the principal mode of communication. Let's discuss each one briefly:

Criticism. A criticism is different from a complaint. Whereas a complaint addresses a specific incident ("You left the toilet seat up"), a criticism is more of a global comment on someone's character or personality ("You left the toilet seat up again, you inconsiderate lout").

Contempt. This is the worst of the four horsemen because it conveys disgust and the sense that you are better than the other person. Sarcasm, name-calling, eye-rolling, "yeah whatever" and mockery all fall within this category. Quite possibly the most potent way to kill a nascent relationship.

Defensiveness. Contrary to intuition, trying to prove yourself right when someone levels a criticism at you does not have the desired effect of making your partner back down. Gottman says this is because "defensiveness is a way to blame your partner," stating in effect that "I'm not the problem – *you* are."

Defensiveness is a disease of the ego. Recall belief #1 about the self from earlier in the book: *Upholding my own importance is a waste of energy.* Much better to adopt the Taoist policy of defenselessness. As Lao Tzu states in Chapter 20 of the *Tao Te Ching*:

> *Stop thinking, and end your problems.*
> *What difference between yes and no?*
> *What difference between success and failure?*
> *Must you value what others value,*
> *Avoid what others avoid?*

How ridiculous!

Also, if you're taken anatta (no-self) to heart and applied Don Miguel Ruiz's Second Agreement to heart – take nothing personally – then this issue dissolves entirely.

Stonewalling. This is avoiding confrontation altogether and tuning out. Men tend to use this tactic more than women, but it's important that you be aware of it nonetheless. When you do this, you're devaluing the partner, conveying in essence that "what you are trying to communicate to me no longer matters," which in essence means that *he* no longer matters. Better at the very least to stay engaged and attentive, even if you don't agree with what he's saying.

So keep your eyes open for unannounced guest appearances of the four horsemen in your relationship, both in yourself and your partner. And if you see criticism, contempt, defensiveness or stonewalling coming up *early* in a relationship, when both people are supposed to be putting their best foot forward, let that be a sign for you to consider reconsidering things.

Some principles for a successful relationship

Entire books have been written on making relationships work, and amongst those, I can't recommend highly enough Gottman's *The Seven Principles for Making Marriage Work*. Everything that he says comes from years of observing real couples and following up with them, so his advice is as good as gold (and the exercises are potentially transformative).

I'm not going to give a summary of the entire book here, but I do want to highlight some salient points he makes about making relationships stronger. His pointers aren't just common sense — they're supercharged common sense, because years of research have proven them to be pivotal. So instead of glossing over this section thinking, "Well that kind of makes sense, I already knew that," think of ways you can actively implement each tip into your relationship. This stuff is the opposite of trivial — it's the difference that makes the difference:

Enhance each other's love maps. This means to engage yourself deeply with the thoughts, beliefs, preferences and feelings of your partner. He's really into sports — do you know what his favorite teams are? Do you know who his best friends are? That he likes his vinaigrette on the side? What his favorite Mexican dish is? What his basic religious beliefs are? What his deepest passions are? The better you know and openly care about these things, the better your relationship will be.

Nurture your fondness and admiration. Every couple starts out with plenty of reasons to like one another. Keep them alive! It becomes the basis for a fundamentally positive view of your partner, which is a useful buffer against future challenges (which will always come). Now I know this sounds totally obvious, but I wouldn't be emphasizing this if I didn't see couples who routinely take each other for granted and allow their relationship to deteriorate. Think of nurturing the fondness and admiration as a potent antidote to the four horsemen mentioned above and the regular workout needed to keep your relationship in shape. Regular compliments, showing interest, propping him up, talking him up to others — all of these little things go a long way.

Know the difference between your solvable and unsolvable problems. If you're a churchgoer and he's an atheist, that's not likely to change – it's an unsolvable problem. Learn to engage in dialogue about it without hurting each other, since the issue ain't going away anytime soon. On the other hand, if you like theater and he prefers baseball, that's a solvable problem. You can alternate which one you watch, go separately with friends, or do something else that you both enjoy.

If you're going to bring up some disgruntlement, it's essential to avoid *harsh startup* – i.e. beginning with an accusatory, blaming tone that devalues your partner. It just starts things on exactly the wrong foot, sending it downhill fast. I really like Gottman's guidelines to ensure your startup is soft:

• Complain but don't blame.
• Make statements that start with "I" instead of "You".
• Describe what's happening without judgment.
• Don't bottle things up.
• Be clear, polite and appreciative.

This section may have been brief, but please do not let its brevity belie the importance of the information contained. It takes only six numbers to win millions in a lottery, so the *quality* of information is often more important than its quantity. What I just gave you was decades of wisdom from someone who's studied thousands of couples, all condensed into a few short paragraphs. Weigh, value and use it accordingly.

Take your own counsel, again

In the end, there are as many ways of keeping a relationship going as there are relationships. What's important is to be aware of *why* you wish to keep a relationship going. It is one thing to keep it going because it's a source of growth and fulfillment for both of you; another to keep it going just for the sake of keeping it going. If something adds to your growth and freedom, you should keep it in your life; if not, let it go. It's a good rule to apply to relationships, and pretty much everything else.

Chapter 13. A New Beginning

What we call the beginning is often the end
And to make an end is to make a beginning.
The end is where we start from.
-- T.S. Eliot, Four Quartets, *Part 4*

When I was seven years old, I had my first crush. Her name was Leila Clark and she was in my second grade class. She was absolutely adorable, so I did nice little things for her whenever possible. Silly little things, like sharing with her one of my home-baked cookies, or letting her cut in front of me in the lunch line. I thought about her all the time and wanted to be her friend so badly and to play with her, but she always remained a bit aloof. I figured maybe she wasn't so into me.

But I was not about to be deterred, so I invited her to my birthday party. Mind you, for a seven year old, the eighth birthday party is the very pinnacle of his life. I was dying for her to come. So I asked, "Leila, wanna come to my birthday party?" She turned around and said, "NO!"

And that was that. It was the year that I got skipped from second grade to the third grade, so soon Leila was out of my class. I never saw her again.

That was over 25 years ago. Now I don't know exactly what would have happened if Leila had said yes on that fateful day. Maybe I still would not have had my first kiss until age 19. Maybe I would not have been scared of girls and utterly mystified by them for the first two decades of my life. But I'll tell you this: on that day, Leila had the power to crown me or crush my little heart. And if she had said yes, maybe, just maybe a little more joy would have been added to the world's storehouses.

I thought of Leila every once in a while – what did she look like now, where did she end up, what was she doing – and in idle moments, enlisted my good friend Google to see if anything turned up, which never did. I mean, she's probably married with 2.3 kids – who knows what her last name is now?

Then came… The Letter.

It popped up in my Facebook account: "Are you the same Alex from my second grade class?" Holy cow. I rubbed my eyes. The sender's name was Leila Clark, and she had an uncanny resemblance to the Leila from second grade – cute little birthmark and all. She was married, a doctor, living in New York, and apparently very pleased to have found me.

So of course, I had to ask her: did she turn me down cold for my eighth birthday party because she didn't like me, or did she actually like me and said no for a different reason? What she wrote back almost broke my heart: "I always liked you, Alex. I just didn't know what to do – I was just a shy little 8-yr old myself! And you were so intimidating!" Intimidating! At eight! I didn't know whether to laugh or cry.

It's true — nobody had taught us what to do then. And the tragedy is that most people go through their entire lives never learning what to when it comes to one of the most important skills in life: connecting meaningfully with another human being. Heaven knows how much deprivation and unrequited love has happened as a result.

A gentle reminder

I've written this book in part to remind you of the power that you already have as a woman. With a single word, you can crown a man the king of the world or crush his dreams. Recognize that you have that power, and use it with compassion towards him and yourself. From Chapter 67 of the *Tao Te Ching*:

> *I have just three things to teach:*
> *Simplicity, patience, compassion.*
> *These three are your greatest treasures.*
> *Simple in actions and in thoughts.*
> *You return to the source of being.*
> *Patient with both friends and enemies,*
> *You accord with the way things are.*
> *Compassionate toward yourself,*
> *You reconcile all beings in the world.*
> *— Lao Tzu, Tao Te Ching, Ch. 67, transl. Stephen Mitchell*

To re-cognize is to see again something that's always been there. And by now, you may have realized that this book is about something more than just dating. It's about recognizing and revealing your inner light to the world. It's about acknowledging yourself as the one-of-a-kind miracle that you are and recognizing that you are a blessing to the planet. It's about recognizing that you are here to experience bliss every glorious day you spend on Earth and to share that with others.

Once you are glowing with bliss, shining your inner light and just plain feeling amazing, the rest has no choice but to fall into place. This is the essence of *wu-wei*, not-doing. There will be no more struggle. There will be no more overthinking. There will just be you, as in Chapter 3 of the *Tao Te Ching*:

> *Practice not-doing,*
> *and everything will fall into place.*

This book is about reminding you of who you really are. You are beauty. You are kindness. You are joy. You are the embodiment of the divine goddess. It's also about reminding you that full effort is full victory. And if you've read this book and found your way to your own inner kindness, joy, and divinity, then you have found fulfillment. As we said in Chapter 2, *the work is the wealth*. Sure, a decent guy would be icing on the cake. But you already possess the cake, and it is you. And if you want someone with whom to share the love, remember this from Williamson:

> *And when a woman remembers her glory, a man of goodwill can barely contain his joy. His real self arises in the presence of her own. I'm telling you, it works, this thing, this looking within to attract what is without. Make room for love, and it always comes. Make a nest for love, and it always settles. Make a home for the beloved, and he will find his way there.*
> – A Woman's Worth, *p. 75*

One day, you will realize that I haven't talked about anything that you didn't already know. And maybe then you will think of these lines from the concluding stanza of T.S. Eliot's *Four Quartets*:

> *We shall not cease from exploration*
> *And the end of all our exploring*
> *Will be to arrive where we started*
> *And know the place for the first time.*

I wish you success in your journey of self-discovery.

Alex Benzer, M.D.
Los Angeles, January 2009

References

Baker, R. and Bellis, M.A. (1990). Do females promote sperm competition? Data for humans. *Animal Behavior* 40: 997-999.

Barash, David P. and Lipton, Judith E. (2001). *The Myth of Monogamy: Fidelity and Infidelity in Animals and People.* New York: W. H. Freeman.

Bargh, John A. et al. (1996). Automaticity of social behavior: direct effects of trait construct and stereotype activation on action. *Journal of Personality and Social Psychology* 71: 230-244.

Becker, A. E. (2004). Television, disordered eating, and young women in Fiji: negotiating body image and identity during rapid social change. *Culture, Medicine and Psychiatry* 28: 533-59.

Beckwith, Michael Bernard (2008). *Spiritual Liberation: Fulfilling Your Soul's Potential.* Oregon: Atria Books/Beyond Words

Brehm, S. et al. (2002) *Intimate Relationships, 3rd Edition.* New York: McGraw-Hill.

Castañeda, Carlos (1993). *The Art of Dreaming.* New York: HarperCollins.

Czikszentmihaly, Mihaly (1991). *Flow: The Psychology of Optimal Experience.* New York: Harper Perennial.

Deida, David (1995). *Intimate Communion: Awakening Your Sexual Essence.* Deerfield Beach, Florida: Health Communications, Inc.

Douglas, Nik and Slinger, Penny (1999). *Sexual Secrets: The Alchemy of Ecstasy, Twentieth Anniversary Edition.* New York: Destiny Books.

Dutton, D.G. and Aron, A. (1974). Some evidence for heightened sexual attraction under conditions of high anxiety. *Journal of Personality and Social Psychology* 30: 510-517.

Fisher, Helen (2004). *Why We Love: The Nature and Chemistry of Romantic Love.* New York: Henry Holt & Co.

Fisher, Helen (1994). *The Anatomy of Love: A Natural History of Mating, Marriage and Why We Stray.* New York: Ballantine Books.

Frankl, Viktor (1959). *Man's Search for Meaning.* Boston: Beacon Press.

Freedman, J.L. and Fraser, S.C. (1966). Compliance without pressure: the foot-in-the-door technique. *Journal of Personality and Social Psychology* 4: 195-203.

Gibran, Kahlil (1923). *The Prophet.* New York: Alfred A. Knopf.

Gilbert, D.T., & Ebert, J.E.J. (2002). Decisions and revisions: The affective forecasting of changeable outcomes. *Journal of Personality and Social Psychology* 82: 503-514.

Gladwell, Malcolm (2000). *The Tipping Point: How Little Things Can Make a Big Difference.* New York: Little, Brown and Co.

Gladwell, Malcolm (2004). *Blink: The Power of Thinking Without Thinking.* New York: Little, Brown and Company.

Gosling, Samuel D. et al. (2002). A room with a cue: personality judgments based on offices and bedrooms. *Journal of Personality and Social Psychology* 82: 379-398.

Gottman, John M. and Silver, N. (1999) *The Seven Principles for Making Marriage Work: A Practical Guide from the Country's Foremost Relationship Expert.* New York: Three Rivers Press.

Hadley, Josie and Staudacher, Carol (1985). *Hypnosis for Change: A Practical Manual of Proven Hypnotic Techniques.* New York: Ballantine Books.

Hume, R.E., trans. (1931) *The Thirteen Principal Upanishads,* 2nd ed. London: Oxford University Press.

"J" (1969). *The Sensuous Woman.* New York: Dell.

Kant, Immanuel (1785). *Grounding for the Metaphysics of Morals.* New York: Hackett.

Kasl, Charlotte (1999). *If the Buddha Dated: A Handbook for Finding Love on a Spiritual Path.* New York: Penguin Compass.

Kellerman, J. et al. (1989). Looking and loving: the effects of mutual gaze on feelings of romantic love. *Journal of Research in Personality* 23: 145-161.

Kosfeld, M. et al. (2005). Oxytocin increases trust in humans. *Nature* 435: 673-6.

Lieberman, David (2000). *Get Anyone to Do Anything: Never Feel Powerless Again – With Psychological Secrets to Control and Influence Every Situation.* New York: St. Martin's Griffin.

Lowndes, Leil (1996). *How to Get Anyone to Fall In Love With You.* Chicago: Contemporary Books.

Moore, M.M. (1985). Nonverbal courtship patterns in women: context and consequences. *Ethology and Sociobiology* 6:237-247.

Morreall, John (1983). *Taking Laughter Seriously.* Albany: State University of New York.

Morris, Desmond (2002). *Peoplewatching: the Desmond Morris Guide to Body Language.* London: Vintage.

Miller, Geoffrey (2002). *The Mating Mind: How Sexual Choice Shaped the Evolution of Human Nature.* New York: Anchor

References

Books.

Mitchell, Stephen (1988). *Tao Te Ching: A New English Version.* New York: HarperCollins Publishers.

Myers, D.G. and Diener, E. (1995). Who is happy? *Psychological Science* 6: 10-19.

Neville (1941). *Your Faith Is Your Fortune.* Camarillo: DeVorss Publications.

NLP Comprehensive Team (1994). *NLP: The New Technology of Achievement.* New York: Quill William Morrow.

Penton-Voak, I.S and Perrett, D.I. (1999). Male facial attractiveness: perceived personality traits and shifting female preferences for male traits across the menstrual cycle. *Advances in the Study of Behavior* 30:219–259.

Post, S. and Neimark, J. (2008). *Why Good Things Happen to Good People: How to Live a Longer, Healthier, Happier Life by the Simple Act of Giving.* New York: Broadway.

Pryor, Karen (1999). *Don't Shoot the Dog: The New Art of Teaching and Training, Revised Edition.* New York: Bantam Books.

Ridley, Matthew (2003). *The Red Queen: Sex and the Evolution of Human Nature.* New York: Ballantine Books.

Ruiz, Don Miguel (1997). *The Four Agreements: A Practical Guide to Personal Freedom.* San Rafael: Amber-Allen.

Sedikides, C., and Strube, M.J. (1997). Self-evaluation: to thine own self be good, to thine own self be true, and to thine own self be better. In M. Zanna (Ed.), *Advances in Experimental Social Psychology.* San Diego: Academic Press.

Swann, W.B., Jr. and Ely, R.J. (1984). A battle of wills: Self-verification versus behavioral confirmation. *Journal of Personality and Social Psychology* 46: 1287-1302.

Tracy, Brian (1993). *Maximum Achievement: Strategies and Skills that Will Unlock Your Hidden Powers to Succeed.* New York: Simon and Schuster.

Williamson, Marianne (1993). *A Woman's Worth.* New York: Ballantine Books.

Williamson, Marianne (1992). *A Return to Love: Reflections on the Principles of 'A Course in Miracles'.* New York: HarperCollins.

Williamson, Marianne (1999). *Enchanted Love: The Mystical Power of Intimate Relationships.* New York: Simon & Schuster.

Wilson, Robert Anton (1999). *Prometheus Rising, 2nd edition.* Tempe, Arizona: New Falcon Publications.

Walster, E. et al. (1978). *Equity Theory and Research.* Boston: Allyn & Bacon.

Walster Hatfield, E. (1965). The effect of self-esteem on romantic liking. *Journal of Experimental Social Psychology* 1: 184-197.